Children Who Read Early

A Publication of
The Horace Mann–Lincoln Institute of School Experimentation
Teachers College, Columbia University

Children Who Read Early

TWO LONGITUDINAL STUDIES

Dolores Durkin

University of Illinois

Teachers College Press

Teachers College, Columbia University

New York, 1966

Printed in the United States of America

To my
Mother
who has always been
a very special friend

Acknowledgments

No researcher works alone. When the research is longitudinal, the people who give assistance are innumerable. Consequently only a few individuals will be named here; but to all who helped with the two studies of early readers, this writer extends sincere appreciation.

William A. Brownell, Dean Emeritus of the School of Education at the University of California, merits the first note of thanks. His enthusiastic response to the initial research proposal was especially heartening for someone who was a relatively new researcher. Here, too, this writer acknowledges both the interest and the practical help of Professor David H. Russell, also of the University of California but now deceased. It is surely true that the respect of Oakland public school personnel for Professor Russell had much to do with the granting of permission to use their schools for longitudinal research that would involve a large number of children. The cooperation of the Oakland schools during all the years of the study was both steady and enthusiastic. So, too, was the assistance of the many University of California students who helped so graciously and efficiently with the administration of tests.

When the researcher, and thus the research, moved to New York City, others were ready to help. Here, the first word of thanks is extended to Dr. Arthur W. Foshay, Director of the Horace Mann–Lincoln Institute of School Experimentation, at Teachers College, Columbia University. It was as a Research Associate in the Institute that this writer was able to begin the second study in New York, and to continue with the initial study in California. During the five-year period of membership in the Institute, special research assistance came from Helen Hanesian, Valora Nelson, Joanne Nurss, and Inez Baker. But to all the other graduate students at Teachers College who gave intermittent help with test administration and statistical analyses, this writer says, "Thank you."

Appreciation also is expressed to personnel in the New York City public schools—first, for permission to do the second study in their schools and, secondly, for their continuous help during the three-year period of that study.

A very special note of gratitude is extended to Professor Walter H. MacGinitie for his careful critique of the report in manuscript; and another to Professor Rosedith Sitgreaves for her assistance with decisions relating to analysis of the data.

Finally, a more general feeling of gratitude is felt for the experience of doing these two studies and, especially, for the opportunity to talk at length with so many parents of young children. It is doubtful that any subsequent research ever will surpass these two studies in the learning opportunities they provided this writer. Hopefully, she will profit from all she has learned about reading—and about people and life in general.

July, 1965   Dolores Durkin

Contents

List of Tables

Children Who Read Early

Chapter I

Introduction

It has been said that curiosity killed a cat. It could also be said that curiosity led to the two studies of early readers described in this report.

In 1957, while a member of the University of California faculty, this writer was engaged in case-study research requiring frequent observations in a first-grade classroom. As a by-product, the research led to a chance encounter with a child discovered to be already reading, even though school instruction in reading had not yet begun. Subsequent testing, requested by the classroom teacher, indicated that this six-year-old girl by the name of Midge had a Stanford–Binet IQ of 148 and a reading achievement grade level of 4.2. Later, a very informal interview with Midge's parents also revealed that she was an only child and a curious child, and that her pre-first-grade achievement in reading resulted from answers that had been given to her frequent queries about words.

According to the parents, Midge deliberately concealed her early reading ability, both in kindergarten and in first grade, because of a desire to be like other children and to do what they were doing. And reading was *not* what other children were doing, either in the kindergarten or in the beginning weeks of first grade, in 1956 and 1957. These years were part of an era in which the official and, apparently, the accepted responsibility of kindergarten was the promotion of social and emotional development. The years 1956 and 1957 also were part of an era in which the beginning weeks of first grade, sometimes even the entire first semester of first grade, was a time for developing reading readiness. As it happened, it was during the sixth week of one such readiness program that Midge was found reading the title pages and the captions in a reading readiness workbook.

1

The incongruity of what Midge brought to first grade, and what the first-grade program offered her, provoked in the writer much curiosity about other early readers who might be in other first grades. More generally, the incongruity provoked questions about the whole matter of readiness for learning to read. Consequently, the professional literature was studied in order to trace the roots and the development of the concepts of readiness in general and reading readiness in particular, and to uncover research that might have been done on the topic of pre-school reading.

What was learned from this survey of the literature, made in 1957, will be presented here. What was learned from the writer's subsequent studies of early readers in California and, later, in New York, will be reported in the chapters that follow.

The Concept of Readiness

At a common-sense level, a relationship between readiness and new learnings is taken for granted. In fact, acceptance of the relationship is frequently reflected in the everyday comments of parents. For instance, the mother who says to her four-year-old, "You can't have a two-wheeler yet because you're too little; you'd only fall," certainly accepts the fundamental importance of readiness for successful performance. So, too, does the mother of a much younger son who says to her husband, "Put a pillow behind Paul's back or he'll topple over."

Most often, in these everyday kinds of situations, readiness is thought of in terms of one variable or a combination of variables that might include, for example, chronological age, parentage, maturation, interest, intelligence, or prior learnings. These same kinds of variables also figure in the professional literature about readiness and the sources from which the concept developed.

This literature is vast. One way to organize the many articles and books is to see their content as part of the long and very familiar discussion about the roles of nature and of nurture in affecting what any human being is or becomes. Within such a framework, then, readiness is a dimension of the classical nature–nurture controversy.

One extreme point of view in this controversy would conceive of readiness as a single-factor phenomenon, unequivocally the result of genetic constitution. In this *genotype* concept, heredity dominates. Heredity determines what any individual is ready to do, to learn, to become.

At the opposite extreme is the *phenotype* concept of readiness. Here, readiness is viewed as the product of learning; it is the result of interaction with an environment that includes, at various times, different combinations of opportunity and deprivation.

While it is easy to describe the two extreme beliefs in the nature–nurture debate, it is much more difficult to identify individuals, either psychologists or educators, who fit neatly and unquestionably into either of these opposite schools of thought. After much searching and careful study, this writer concludes that although certain eminent investigators have strongly emphasized the unique importance of heredity or, as the case may be, environment, none has ever really maintained that either heredity or environment is the *only* factor that affects the general development and the specific abilities of an individual.

Some might say that the psychologist John Watson came closest to promoting an extreme position, a position clearly portrayed in the famous quotation from his book of 1924, *Behaviorism:*

> Give me a dozen healthy infants, well-formed, and my own specified world to bring them up in and I'll guarantee to take any one at random and train him to become any type of specialist I might select—doctor, lawyer, artist, merchant-chief and, yes, even beggarman and thief, regardless of his talents, penchants, tendencies, abilities, vocations, and race of his ancestors. [99:82] [1]

Even in the case of Watson, however, a question must be raised about whether he really believed environment to be the only factor affecting development, or whether his strongly stated position was simply an attempt to counteract the very special prominence given to heredity, and even to instincts, by other leading psychologists of his time. For it certainly can be said that the early years of this twentieth century paid special homage to genetic constitution as the most important factor in determining what any individual was ready to do, to learn, to become. What are the sources of this view of man?

A study of the literature of the early years of the twentieth century points to the striking influence of the psychologist G. Stanley Hall. And Hall, as is evident in his many writings, was a staunch believer in the unique importance of heredity. In fact, a book about his writings, written by Partridge in 1912, is appropriately entitled *Genetic Philosophy of Education* [78].

Hall's own writings, coupled with the writings of others about Hall, indicate that his beliefs regarding man and his development had both historical and conceptual roots in Darwin's theory of evolution [20, 82]. Here, some recent comments of J. McV. Hunt recall the implications of Darwin's theory for psychology:

> . . . Darwin believed that evolution took place, not by changes wrought through use or disuse as Lamarck had thought, but by changes resulting from variations in the progeny of every species. . . . Implicit in this notion was the assumption that the characteristics of any organism are predetermined by the genetic constitution with which the organism comes into being. . . . [49:210]

[1] Numbers in brackets identify the numbered references on pages 143–147. Page numbers are shown, after a colon, when a reference is quoted directly.

Quite clearly, Hall subscribed to a belief in the unique importance of genetic constitution. He also promoted, as a kind of parallel thinking, the doctrine of recapitulation. Note the following quotation, for example:

> The most general formulation of all the facts of development that we yet possess is contained in the law of recapitulation. This law declares that the individual, in his development, passes through stages similar to those through which the race has passed, and in the same order. [41:8]

Hall's belief in a concept of man that emphasizes a predetermined nature which unfolds in stages had a pronounced effect on the thinking of his students. And these students included people like Frederick Kuhlmann, Lewis Terman, and Arnold Gesell. Because Gesell's work bears so directly on the concept of readiness, it deserves special attention in this review of the literature.

Gesell, of course, was a physician, and so his great interest in the maturation process is not unexpected. His many studies of children, and, in turn, the studies of his students, always emphasized normative data about maturation [35, 36, 38]. In these studies the concern was for the average or typical child: the developmental stages through which he passes and, equally important, the age at which he passes from one growth stage into another.

In describing, and also in explaining, the development of the various stages, Gesell referred not to such factors as learning and practice but, instead, to such sources as "intrinsic growth" and "neural ripening." This concept of development found support in the earlier writings of E. L. Thorndike in which readiness for learning was discussed in terms of brain physiology and the behavior of neurones [93]. Such a concept of development also found support in empirical studies of animals— studies in which, typically, the animal was quite low on the phylogenetic scale. Probably the best known of these studies were those done by Coghill, in the 1920's, on the development of behavior in amblystoma [18]. Commenting on Coghill's animal studies, J. McV. Hunt has written:

> These [studies] demonstrated that behavioral development, like anatomical development, starts at the head-end and proceeds tailward, starts from the inside and proceeds outward, and consists of progressive differentiation of more specific units from general units. From such evidence Coghill and others inferred the special additional notion that behavior unfolds automatically as the anatomical basis for behavior matures. [49:213]

An emphasis on "unfolding behavior" also appeared in studies of children [36, 68]. In these studies, the factor of time came to be seen as the remedy for a lack of maturity or readiness. Here, the findings of McGraw's research with twin boys are typical, both in content and in the way they were interpreted and applied [68]. In this widely publicized research of the early 1930's, McGraw attempted to assess the effect of practice on the development of motor skills during infancy. McGraw's two subjects were twin boys. Over time, one twin was given frequent opportunities to practice such motor skills as crawling, while the other twin was not. Findings in the study regarding the age at which each twin mastered the various motor skills led McGraw to conclude that practice does not hasten the developmental process. Or, to use the terminology of Gesell and others, neural ripening seemed to remain uninfluenced by environmental factors.

Throughout the 1920's and the 1930's, McGraw and other researchers who were concerned with motor development in children commonly used their data to counteract the extreme environmental position of John Watson and his school of behaviorism. The data about motor skills also were used, however, to describe and even to explain the development of intellectual skills. In fact, many would say that the progressive education movement, very popular at this time, was much influenced by the doctrine of neural ripening. John Watson, for example, wrote the following in 1928:

> Professor John Dewey and many other educators have been insisting for the last twenty years upon a method of training which allows the child to develop from within. This is really a doctrine of mystery. [100:40]

In later years another psychologist, David Ausubel, commented:

> According to this [progressive education] point of view, the educational environment facilitates development best by providing a maximally permissive field that does not interfere with the predetermined process of spontaneous maturation. [6:27]

It is easy to understand how a concept like "reading readiness," especially when interpreted in terms of a need to postpone reading instruction, fitted very naturally into the progressive education setting, and into the thinking of researchers like Gesell and McGraw. Actually, though, since the very beginning of the century, other kinds of factors were at work which also fostered the belief that children needed more time to get ready to learn to read.

The Concept of Reading Readiness

In the early 1900's, children started first grade at the age of six. And first grade and first steps in reading went together. This use of a chronological age of six as the criterion for starting reading was not without its critics, to be sure. Among the most influential was John Dewey. Early in the century, Edmund B. Huey, a well-known follower of Dewey, advocated a postponed start in his 1908 text, *The Psychology and Pedagogy of Reading,* pointing out that Dewey himself had suggested the age of eight as an appropriate time to begin school instruction in reading [47:304].

To understand fully the reasoning of these men, it is important to remember that both were reacting as much against the way reading was taught as they were against the age at which reading was begun. Dewey characterized school instruction in reading as passive and mechanical [47]. Huey said it was unnatural, and devoted a whole chapter of his text to a description of the more natural ways in which children could begin to read at home. His comments about the preschool child's "natural, everyday activities" sound very modern, although they were made in 1908:

> The child makes endless questionings about the names of things, as every mother knows. He is concerned also about the printed notices, signs, titles, visiting cards, etc., that come in his way, and should be told what these "say" when he makes inquiry. It is surprising how large a stock of printed or written words a child will gradually come to recognize in this way. [47:314]

Later on, but still in the early years of the century, school surveys became extremely popular and were, consequently, extremely numerous. The reports of the surveys were consistent in pointing to the large numbers of children who were failing first grade, generally because of inadequate achievement in reading.

The reaction to the findings of the school surveys was one of great and wide concern. Reflecting the concern was the recommendation of the National Society for the Study of Education that schools develop a period of preparation for reading. *The Twenty-Fourth Yearbook* of the Society, published in 1925, gives the following description of the preparation period:

> This period includes the pre-school age, the kindergarten, and frequently the early part of the first grade. Its primary purpose is to provide the training and experience which prepare pupils for reading. [75:24]

Apparently the NSSE's emphasis on the need for special early experiences to insure more successful reading was overshadowed by the more popular view which emphasized time, or "neurological ripeness," as the remedy for insufficient readiness.

Apparently, too, the NSSE recommendation was also surrounded by a kind of thinking that was very much engrossed in measuring and testing. The educational literature of the 1920's is filled with research reports citing the correlation between intelligence (or mental age) and the reading achievement of first-grade children [25, 46, 85]. A survey of this literature prompts the suggestion that all of these reports were preparing fertile ground for quick and uncritical acceptance of the study by Morphett and Washburne, published in 1931 [73], in which the recommendation was made that a mental age of 6.5 is a prerequisite for success in beginning reading. Although many questions should have been raised about the quality and especially about the general applicability of the Morphett–Washburne research, its findings, implying the need to postpone and to wait, were a "natural" for the early 1930's. They won the quick support both of professional educators and of many psychologists. As a result, professional texts written for reading methods courses soon were proclaiming that school instruction in reading should be postponed until a mental age level of 6.5 is reached [19, 42, 61].

Meanwhile, though, there was some loss of faith in the power of an IQ or MA to predict readiness for reading. The disenchantment, however, was still accompanied by a great faith in testing. Consequently, much interest began to develop in the possibility of constructing reading readiness tests. The interest first appears in the literature in the latter part of the 1920's [8, 22, 89]. Here, a 1927 editorial in *Childhood Education* is helpful in portraying the beliefs of the time:

> In the field of reading it is essential that a joyous attitude of success shall be cultivated from the first. This necessitates a stage of development in which the learner is capable of getting meaning from the crooked marks which symbolize ideas. When does this period come? . . . In which direction shall we look to discover the truth regarding this confused situation? Fortunately the scientific method points the way toward the solution of this as of other baffling problems. The first steps have been taken. First, the problem has been recognized. Second, a name has been coined for the characteristic which is sought, Reading Readiness, a term not only alliterative but meaningful. Third, tests are in process of developing which shall be applicable to any young child. . . . So we may look forward to the day when the measure of readiness will rest in objective tests and parent and teacher will both be governed thereby. [54:209]

The reading readiness tests that were soon described in the literature, and that were later used in classrooms, were followed by many studies attempting to evaluate their effectiveness as predictors of success in reading. One of the best and most comprehensive of the studies was done by Arthur Gates and his associates [34]. This particular study, begun in 1934 and published five years later, "was designed to test the value of practically every type of test, rating, examination, or other means of appraisal which has been suggested, or which the authors could think of, as a means of predicting reading progress." One of its conclusions is particularly well worth repeating here: "It should be noted that among the tests of little or no predictive value are many tests and ratings widely recommended in books and articles on reading readiness testing and teaching."

This negative note—and there were many more to come—had some effect on the content of subsequent readiness tests but little effect on the number of tests published. In fact, together with reading readiness workbooks, the tests became a routine part of the beginning materials in basal reader series.

It should be pointed out here that studies questioning the predictive value of readiness tests were not the only kind to receive scant acclaim in the 1930's. Again, the research of Gates and his students is illustrative. Certain of their studies focused on the relationship between varied methods of instruction and first-grade reading achievement. Reported at a time when a mental age of 6.5 generally was accepted as a requirement for success in beginning reading, the findings are especially interesting. One research report, for example, describes four different methods of teaching reading and the achievement that resulted from each method. Commenting on the findings, Gates writes: "Reading is begun by very different materials, methods, and general procedures, some of which a pupil can master at the mental age of five with reasonable ease, others of which would give him difficulty at the mental age of seven" [31].

In another research report, Gates and his associates write: "Correlations of mental age with reading achievement at the end of the year were about 0.25. When one studies the range of mental ages from the lowest to the highest in relation to reading achievement, there appears no suggestion of a crucial or critical point above which very few fail and below which a relatively large proportion fail" [33]. The same report concludes that "the optimum time of beginning reading is not entirely dependent upon the nature of the child himself, but it is in a large measure determined by the nature of the reading program."

From these studies, of course, a concept of reading readiness emerged which emphasized, not the unique significance of mental age or of maturation, but, rather, the very special importance of the kind of reading instruction offered a child. It should not be surprising, therefore, that relatively little attention was given to the Gates studies at the time of their publication in the late 1930's. The findings simply did not move with the stream of popular thought. Nor, it seems, were the studies able to redirect the current of the stream; for the reading readiness literature throughout the 1940's, and even into the 1950's, continued to be concerned with maturation, with mental age, and with the assessment of readiness by means of reading readiness tests.

During those two decades, the psychological literature most frequently quoted pertained to the Gesell studies, which were still very popular, and which were being continued by Gesell's students [53]. Another psychologist popular among educators was Willard Olson, who, throughout this period, was describing the development of a child in terms of "organismic age" [76, 77]. Robert Havighurst also became well known as he discussed the growth of an individual in terms of "developmental tasks" [43].

Occasionally, of course, there was a dissenter. One of the most vocal critics in education was Glenn McCracken, who in the early 1950's began writing professional protests against the use of the readiness concept to de-emphasize the ineffectiveness of school instruction in reading [64, 65, 66]. Had McCracken's complaints been calm and carefully substantiated, they might have been taken more seriously. As it was, McCracken's articles and his subsequent book, *The Right to Learn* [67], were viewed more as the writings of a crank than as a reason for serious reexamination of the school's use of the readiness concept. And so, as the literature clearly shows, questions and discussions about reading readiness—even in the 1950's—continued to focus on maturation, mental age, and readiness testing. Too often overlooked was the possibility that changes in instruction might affect a child's readiness to begin to read.

Research on Preschool Reading Achievement

With this review of the literature in the background, it should not come as any great surprise that an attempt made in 1957 to uncover research on preschool reading met with a minimum of success. A few relevant books and articles were found, but in terms of research the topic of early reading seemed to have been neglected almost to the point of total omission.

The research that stands out—and it is highly visible primarily because of the uncommon focus—is a study done by Davidson in 1931 [21]. Subjects in Davidson's research were 13 children, each with a mental age of four years. Chronologically, the children were divided into three-, four-, and five-year-old groups. The purpose of Davidson's study was to find out, first, whether children with a mental age of only four years could learn to read, and, second, whether bright, average, and dull children, all with this same mental age, would learn to read equally well under the same experimental conditions.

Each of Davidson's 13 subjects received ten minutes of reading instruction every day for a period of four and one-half months. At the end of this period, reading tests were administered. Results showed that all the children had learned to read some words; the most successful child identified 269 words, while the least successful read 20 words. Test results also showed that the bright three-year-olds were superior in achievement to the older children.

In Davidson's research no systematic attempt was made to examine the reading progress of the 13 subjects as they became older and entered school. The report of the research indicates, however, that there were informal contacts with some of the children, and that they showed continued success with reading. Although Davidson writes that "This record of achievement tends to refute a not uncommon belief that early training in reading is injurious to children," there was no carefully gathered evidence in the research report to warrant any generalizations about the effect of earlier reading on later achievement. Davidson's study simply showed that children younger than six could be taught to read and that mental age seemed more important than chronological age in the achievement that resulted from the reading instruction given.

The survey of the literature uncovered two other reports of children who learned to read before the age of six, and in settings other than a classroom. The first of these appeared in a 1918 issue of the *Journal of Applied Psychology* [3], and was written by a parent who remains anonymous as he tells how he helped his young daughter learn to read. According to his account, the child was reading fluently at 26 months. The report begins with an introduction by Lewis Terman in which he mentions having urged this parent to write about the early reading achievement of his daughter.

Another report of early reading appears in an unpublished master's thesis completed by Brown in 1924 [12]. The initial part of the thesis describes the successful efforts of the author to teach two three-year-olds to identify written words. The teaching sessions took place in the homes of the children over a period of three months.

The second part of this same thesis describes the efforts of the author to teach two groups of preschool children to begin to read. The chronological age of the 13 children in the two groups ranged from 22 months to 5 years 11 months. In describing the results of her work with the two groups, Brown notes that "In no case did a child not learn to recognize some words." Brown also writes, in concluding her report, that "striking individual differences in temperament, training, and environment determine, for each individual child, the age at which formal instruction should begin."

A study by Wilson, reported in 1938, describes early help with reading given in a school setting [102], in connection with the development of a curriculum for four- and five-year-old children attending the Horace Mann School at Teachers College, Columbia University. Emphasized in Wilson's report is the fact that the reading instruction was carried on "without violating in any way the basic emphasis on a varied and rich experience for young children or . . . the ideal of individualized learning." There is no indication of attempts to trace the later reading progress of the children who began to read as a result of informal instruction in nursery school and kindergarten.

Another study, reported by Almy in 1949, bears some relationship to earlier reading—but in a way that is different from the Davidson, Brown, and Wilson studies [1]. Almy's research was concerned with the relationship between a child's success with reading in first grade, and the kinds of experiences the child had at home during the previous year. In this study, reading achievement was measured by tests administered to 106 first-grade children during the final month of the school year, and by teachers' ratings of their achievement. The kinds of experiences the children had during their fifth year were identified and described in parent interviews carried on when the subjects were in first grade.

A problem for Almy's study was the large number of subjects who "failed to make an appreciable score on the [reading] tests." Nonetheless, Almy still concluded that the best readers in the group of 106 were "children whose experiences in kindergarten, in play, and with adults had in them some elements of reading." In this study, "experience with an element of reading" was defined very broadly; it included being read to as well as attempts at actual instruction in reading.

The other studies—as of 1957—that have some bearing on preschool reading only tell about the retrospective accounts of older subjects who were both intellectually gifted and skillful in reading. The first of the three studies in this group is Terman's well-known research with gifted children. In a 1925 publication, Terman mentions that 250 of his 552 subjects reported having learned to read before starting school [92]. Of these, 113 said they learned before the age of five; 34, before they were four; and 9, before they were three. The remaining subjects who said they read early were unable to recall when the reading began.

Strang, in a more recent study, examined the reading autobiographies of 54 junior high school students who had IQ's of 120 or higher [90]. In the report of her findings, she writes that "about half . . . said they learned to read when they were five years old or younger." Strang also noted that "a few somehow learned all by themselves to associate printed words with meanings."

In the third study of this retrospective kind, Kasdon examined the backgrounds of 50 superior readers among college freshmen [55]. On the basis of questionnaire data, Kasdon reported that 27 of these 50 superior readers said they read before entering first grade. Of the remaining 23 subjects, 14 thought they learned to read during first grade, and the rest could not recall when they first started.

Conclusions from the Survey of Research Literature

What was known about preschool reading achievement in 1957, the year this writer found a child by the name of Midge who entered first grade reading at a fourth-grade level?

The eight reports described above, taken one at a time or as a group, represent a very limited study of early reading. One was merely a parental account of how a single preschool child began to read. Four group studies were concerned with early reading only in an indirect way, and in three of these the data reported were based solely on the recollections of older subjects about their abilities as three-, four-, and five-year-old children.

Preschool reading was the central focus of three studies. In those of Davidson and Brown, the number of subjects was very small. That of Wilson was concerned more with the development of appropriate ways to teach reading to pre-first-grade children than with the exact amount of achievement that resulted from the instruction. In none of these studies was an effort made to follow the early readers after they entered first grade.

Together, it seems fair to say, the findings of the eight reports merely show that some children can be taught to read before the age of six in both school and out-of-school situations; that preschool experiences having in them some elements of reading can have a positive effect on first-grade achievement in reading; and that among groups of gifted adults who are superior readers, some report having learned to read before the first grade.

Because this 1957 review of the literature turned up so little information about early reading, the writer began planning for the present research. The result of the planning was two longitudinal studies. The first began in September, 1958, and was terminated six years later, in June, 1964. The second began in September of 1961, and was also terminated in June of 1964. Both studies are reported in the chapters that follow.

Chapter **II**

The First Study:
Oakland, California

The first study was designed to examine early reading achievement in a somewhat general way. With practically no prior research to serve as a guideline, this initial study could best be described as exploratory. Central questions were as follows:

How many children learn to read at home and, as a result, enter first grade already reading?

What is the effect of this early ability on a child's future achievement in reading?

What kinds of factors promote early reading, and do they have implications for school instruction in reading?

Population for the Study

Interest in the relative frequency of pre-first-grade reading achievement required, at least ideally, that a total first-grade population be tested in reading at the very beginning of the school year. Ideally, too, this first-grade population should be part of a school system neither too small nor too atypical. For these reasons, the Oakland, California, public schools were selected for the first study.

According to 1950 census data, Oakland had a population of 384,575 [14]. This population also was described as being 14.5 per cent non-white. Because of the size of Oakland, and because of its proximity both to industry and to colleges and a state university, the city was heterogeneous in terms of social class distribution. A lack of private schools of the kind that attract members of the upper classes also meant that children from a great variety of backgrounds would be attending the public schools.

In 1958, the year the first study began, the Oakland public school system included 64 elementary schools. In these 64 schools there were 183 first-grade classrooms.

As it turned out, three of the Oakland elementary schools did not participate in the study. A school for physically handicapped children was excluded as being atypical; and principals in two other elementary schools were not willing to participate in the study. Together, the 61 schools that did participate had a first-grade population of 5,236 children.

When the 61 schools were visited, it was found that a total of 37 first-grade children were "repeaters"; they had already spent a year in first grade. Consequently these children did not qualify as potential subjects. School visits also identified 96 children who had attended Oakland kindergartens in which a small amount of help with reading was given toward the end of the kindergarten year. Even though some of these 96 children might have been reading before this kindergarten help began, they were eliminated as possible subjects because the concern of the research was only for early reading that was the product of nonschool learning. As a result, the first-grade population from which early readers were to be sought numbered 5,103 children. Of these, 2,602 were boys and 2,501 were girls.

Test to Identify Subjects

Subjects were identified by a two-step testing procedure. The test that was initially used to find the early readers allowed for the identification of 37 words.[1] These words, typed in large print, were listed in columns and also used in short sentences. (The two arrangements of words were to accommodate children who might find it more natural to read sentences than to read columns of isolated words. A child could respond to either arrangement.) The vocabulary for the test was comprised of all the words that were common to the preprimers of the three basal reader series used most frequently in Oakland schools.[2] Any child who was able to read aloud a minimum of 18 words was considered to be a possible subject for the research.

The use of this short and quick oral test as the first step in identifying early readers resulted from a variety of considerations. First of all, the concern of the research for the frequency of early achievement meant that a large number of children would be tested—5,103 to be exact. In addition, subjects had to be identified at the very start of the first-grade year, before school instruction in reading began. It was also felt that, for young children, an oral individual test would be more reliable and less threatening than a paper-and-pencil test administered to a group.

The decision to use basal reader words in this initial test was based

[1] A copy of the test can be found in Appendix A.

[2] Information about the basal readers used in Oakland schools was supplied by the Director of Elementary School Education.

on the assumption that if a parent deliberately planned to teach his preschool child to read, he probably would use school-like materials. In addition, it was very possible that some of the early readers would have learned some of their vocabulary from the school books of older brothers and sisters.

A basal reader vocabulary is restrictive, of course, especially in its failure to include the words a young child might notice on milk cartons, street signs, TV commercials, and the like. On the other hand, such a vocabulary does include words that commonly appear in all ordinary reading material, regardless of theme—words like *the* and *to*.

The decision to select as subjects only those children who could identify at least 18 of the 37 test words was arbitrary. But all definitions of "reader," as contrasted with "nonreader," are abitrary. At one extreme the term "reader" might be defined as anyone who is able to identify a single word; at another extreme, as anyone who responds fluently to difficult words and long, complicated sentences. For purposes of this research, an "early reader" was initially defined as a beginning first-grade child who was able to identify at least 18 words from a list of 37, and who had not received school instruction in reading. Standardized reading tests would be given to the children who met this requirement. Those children who could not achieve a raw score of at least 1 on the standardized tests would be eliminated from the study.

Identification of Subjects

With the help of fourteen assistants, the initial test of 37 words was administered individually and orally to 5,103 first-grade children. All the testing was done within the first seven days of the school year, before classroom instruction in reading began. Test results indicated that 49 children in 27 schools qualified as possible subjects. Of these 49 children, comprising slightly less than 1 per cent (.0096) of the population tested, 20 were boys and 29 girls. The group consisted of 26 Caucasians, 12 Negroes, and 11 Orientals.

Once identified by means of the quick word-identification test, the 49 children were given selected tests from the 1958 edition of the *Gates Reading Tests.*[3] They first took *Primary Word Recognition* and *Primary Paragraph Reading.* All 49 children were able to score on both of these tests. In fact, 7 received perfect scores on both tests, and consequently were also given *Advanced Primary Word Recognition* and *Advanced Primary Paragraph Reading.*

This testing was completed within the first two weeks of the school year and, again, before classroom instruction in reading began. The

---

[3] Details about the procedures followed in administering the standardized reading tests throughout the six years of the research are given in Chapter III. Here, the intent is to give a very general and very brief description of the subjects, and of the way they were identified.

results were individual median scores ranging from 1.5 to 4.5, on a grade-level norm scale.[4] The median grade score for the total group of 49 subjects at this time was 1.9.

Intelligence Test

After the early readers were identified, a psychometrist began administering the *Revised Stanford–Binet Intelligence Scale,* Form L (1937 Edition). This testing was completed within the first two months of the school year. Here, test results were individual intelligence quotients ranging from 91 to 161. The median intelligence quotient for the group of 49 subjects was 121.[5] At the time the Stanford–Binet test was administered, the subjects had mental ages ranging from 5 years 11 months to 10 years 7 months. The median mental age for the group was 7 years 10 months.

Other Data

Other data about the 49 early readers will be reported in detail in subsequent chapters. For now, though, it may be useful to summarize some information that can be kept in mind as the detailed data are presented. For instance, it may be helpful to remember that of the 49 early readers, only 7 came from families that could be classified as professional or upper-middle class; 15 were of the lower-middle class, while 26 could be classified as upper-lower and 1 as lower-lower class.

It may be helpful to remember, too, that by the end of the first year of this longitudinal study, 12 of the early readers had been double-promoted, and so were preparing to enter third grade rather than second grade. And, finally, it may help to keep in mind that during the six years of this study there were 42 school transfers involving 26 of the subjects, and that by the end of the research the 49 early readers had been in 14 different school systems. All of this is to say that longitudinal research is very difficult indeed, and that it requires the persistence of a sleuth as much as it needs the skills of a researcher.

[4] Each subject's achievement, at each testing period, is described by the median of the grade-levels achieved in whatever tests the subject was qualified to take. The selection of tests for each testing period is described in the next chapter.

[5] The IQ scores achieved by the subjects during this first year are used throughout the research to describe their intelligence.

Chapter III

Reading Achievement in the First Study

One major goal in this research was to study the reading achievement of children who started to read before the first grade. Consequently, plans for the research required decisions about the methods to study this achievement and also about the length of time the study would continue.

One early decision was that reading achievement would be examined during the years the subjects attended elementary school. This amount of time seemed sufficient for a meaningful assessment of the effect of early reading on later achievement. It was also decided that if an early reader was double-promoted during the research period, he would still be considered a subject because the intent of the research was to study reading achievement over time, not over continuous and successively higher grade-levels. The same decision, for the same reason, also held for the subjects who might be retained in a grade for more than one year.

Selection of Reading Tests

Choosing the standardized tests which would trace the progress of the subjects presented some problems because of the scarcity of scaled series of reading tests which have something appropriate both for the beginner and also for the more mature reader. It was assumed that, in research that was to continue for six years, very easy tests would be required initially but at the end of the study some subjects would be well advanced and would need quite difficult tests. The decision was to use the *Gates Reading Tests* (1958 Edition). This series of tests is widely known; it includes tests of varying difficulty; and it had just been revised when plans for the research were being formulated. Specifically, the tests selected were: (1) *Gates Primary Reading Tests—Word Recognition* and *Paragraph Reading;* (2) *Gates Advanced Primary Reading Tests— Word Recognition* and *Paragraph Reading;* and (3) the *Gates Reading Survey.* Form 1 of each of the tests was used throughout the research.

Description of Reading Tests

Two of the easiest tests in the Gates series are *Primary Word Recognition* (PWR) and *Primary Paragraph Reading* (PPR).

The PWR test, as described in the test manual, "consists of 48 exercises, each of which contains four printed words and a picture which illustrates the meaning of one of them. The task is to encircle the word that tells the most about the picture" [32]. Fifteen minutes are allowed. For this test, the scoring procedure penalizes the "guesser" in that the total raw score equals the number of correct responses minus one-third the number of incorrect responses.

The PPR test, as described in the test manual, "consists of 26 paragraphs, each accompanied by illustrations which are to be marked in such a way as to indicate the meaning of the paragraph. Vocabulary and sentence structure of the test units increase gradually in complexity and difficulty, and the successive passages become longer" [32]. Twenty minutes are allowed. In this test, the raw score is the total number of correct responses.

The next pair of tests used in this research consisted of *Advanced Primary Word Recognition* (AWR) and *Advanced Primary Paragraph Reading* (APR). The AWR test, except for its greater difficulty, is like the PWR test, described above. The APR test follows the general form of the PPR test, also described above, but has a total of 32 test items rather than 26.

The third and final level of testing for the research consisted of one test, the *Gates Reading Survey.* This *Survey* includes three subtests: (1) *Speed and Accuracy;* (2) *Reading Vocabulary;* and (3) *Level of Comprehension.* To maintain the pattern of the PWR and PPR tests, and also of the AWR and APR tests, only the subtests *Reading Vocabulary* and *Level of Comprehension* were used in the research.

The *Reading Vocabulary* test requires a child to select from five words the one word which "means the same or nearly the same as the first word in each line." The total raw score equals the number of items correct minus one-fourth the number wrong. The highest possible score on this test is 65.

The *Level of Comprehension* test requires the child to select from a row of five words the one word which "makes the best sense" in sentences from which words have been omitted. In this test, too, the raw score is the number of correct choices minus one-fourth the number of incorrect choices. The highest possible raw score is 43.

A summary of the three pairs of tests just described, and the range of possible grade scores (grade-level norms) for each test, follows:

Test	Grade-Level Range
Primary Word Recognition (PWR)	1.4— 3.7
Primary Paragraph Reading (PPR)	1.4— 4.4
Advanced Primary Word Recognition (AWR)	1.8— 5.8
Advanced Primary Paragraph Reading (APR)	1.8— 6.2
Reading Vocabulary	2.1—12.8
Level of Comprehension	2.1—12.5

Administration of Reading Tests

Each time standardized reading tests were administered during the six-year period of this research, the intent was to identify the upper limits of each subject's achievement in reading. Consequently, the testing procedure was one that allowed for the use of pairs of tests which had appropriate ceilings for each subject at each testing period.

Once subjects were initially identified by means of the 37-word test described in Chapter II, the standardized testing of the 49 subjects began with the PWR and PPR tests. From that point on, however, the tests given to each subject depended on test performance. For all of the testing periods, including the first, the following plan was adhered to by the research assistants who administered the reading tests.

Whenever a subject took the PWR and PPR tests and missed two or fewer items on the more difficult of the two, the PPR test, he then would be given the AWR and APR tests.[1] Whenever a subject took the AWR and APR tests and missed two or fewer items on the more difficult of the two, the APR test, he then would be given the *Reading Vocabulary* and *Level of Comprehension* tests. The assumption, at the beginning of the study, was that these two subtests in the *Survey* would continue to be sufficiently difficult for all of the subjects throughout all the years of the research. Test results at the end of the study indicated the assumption was correct.

At the beginning of the research it was decided that each subject's achievement in reading, at each testing period, would be described by the median of all the grade scores achieved in whatever tests he was qualified to take. The median grade score was selected because it would be a conservative estimate of reading achievement, as achievement was to be measured in the research.

[1] The number of tests administered at one session depended upon the child's interest in the testing, and also upon the ease with which he finished tests. For some children, a research assistant would do part of the testing on one day and the rest on another day.

Testing Periods

The first standardized testing was completed within the first two weeks of the first grade, before school instruction in reading began. Subsequently, testing took place in May of every year, for six years. During each of these testing periods, test administration followed the procedures outlined above. An extra testing session, also following the same procedures, was held at the very beginning of the second year of the study.

The extra session was designed to shed some light on a question raised by a 1941 research report by Keister, in which he maintained that reading skills attained by "under-age" children lack permanence [56]. In his research, Keister studied the reading progress of three groups of first-grade children who were taught to read before they reached a chronological age of six years. The reading achievement of the children was measured at the end of grade one, and then again at the beginning of grade two. On the basis of the test data, Keister concluded that it is possible for "under-age" children to make normal progress in reading during the first year, but that their achievement lacks permanence. Although only limited and conflicting data were available, he also maintained that the loss in reading achievement between grades one and two is not made up in succeeding years.

Of course, the concern of the Keister study was different from that of the present research. Keister's "young" subjects were taught to read in the first grade before they were six, whereas the subjects in this research were "young" readers because they had been doing some reading during the years prior to first grade. The subjects in the present study had had a longer time to live with "learning to read," and so might be learning in a more slowly paced—and, perhaps, self-paced—fashion. In any case, it was in order to reexamine the claim that early reading achievement lacks permanence that the 49 subjects in this study were tested in reading at the end of the first year of the research and again at the beginning of the second year.

The first test data to be reported are those that describe the reading achievement of the 49 subjects over a six-year period. In subsequent sections of the chapter, other data will be reported that describe the reading achievement of the subjects as it compared with the achievement of classmates who did not learn to read before the first grade.

Test Results for Early Readers

Table 1 summarizes reading achievement data for the early readers over the six-year period. It also shows the correlation between achievement and intelligence. Table 2 presents the data from the intelligence testing reported earlier in Chapter II.

Table 1. Reading progress of the early readers over a six-year
period and the relationship between this progress
and their intelligence

Date of Testing	Reading Grade-Level		Correlation between Reading Achievement and Intelligence
	MEDIAN	RANGE	
Sept. 1958 (N=49) (Grade 1.0)	1.9	1.5— 4.5	.40
May 1959 (N=49)	3.7	2.3— 5.6	.64
Sept. 1959 (N=49)	4.0	2.3— 6.5	.71
May 1960 (N=49)	4.9	3.3— 8.9	.80
May 1961 (N=49)	5.3	4.4—10.6	.71
May 1962 (N=49)	6.7	4.8—11.2	.66
May 1963 (N=49)	7.6	5.0—11.7	.79
May 1964 (N=34) a (Grade 6.8)	9.0	5.2—12.3	.70

a Because 15 of the original subjects had been double-promoted, only 34 were
still in elementary school in the last year of the study.

Table 2. Stanford-Binet intelligence data
for the 49 early readers

Subjects	Intelligence Quotient	
	RANGE	MEDIAN
Boys and girls (N=49)	91—161	121
Boys (N=20)	96—151	122
Girls (N=29)	91—161	119

In Table 1, test data for May, 1959, and for September, 1959, are
relevant in considering the claim made by Keister that the achievement
of "young" readers lacks permanence [56]. Here, of course, there is no
suggestion that the Keister study and this present research focused on
the same kind of early reading. Nor is there any pretense to knowledge
of the exact reasons for the levels of achievement shown for May, 1959,
and September, 1959. What the data in Table 1 indicate is simply that
for these 49 subjects there was not the loss in achievement that the Keister
research—at least as it is generally interpreted—would tend to predict.

A more comprehensive look at all the data in Table 1 shows that
children who first learn to read at home do not seem to encounter problems with reading, once school instruction begins. Over a period of six
school years, seven years of growth were made in reading—at least according to group data described by median grade-level scores.

Median grade-level scores for individual subjects, as portrayed in

Table 1 by the ranges of such scores, also are encouraging—although, by the end of the study in May, 1964, three subjects were reading below grade level. In May, 1964, the ninth month of the sixth grade, these three subjects received median grade level scores of 5.2, 5.4, and 5.6. The scores for this small group were atypical for the group of subjects as a whole in that, in May, 1964, the next three lowest median scores for the remaining subjects were 6.9, 7.0, and 7.4.

A variety of factors could account for the relatively low reading scores of the three subjects. One possible factor was the great difficulty of the content in the subtests of the Gates *Survey*, which these subjects were taking in May, 1964. This difficulty was made apparent by the fact that subjects consistently dropped in their grade-level scores as they moved from the level of the AWR and APR tests up to the level of the two subtests in the *Survey*. Another possible reason is that test scores for individuals are less reliable than scores describing group trends. In the case of each of these three children, reading scores at the end of the fifth grade were higher than at the end of the sixth grade.

Other factors that might have affected the reading achievement of these three subjects are summarized below:

Subject	Reading Grade-Level May, 1964	IQ	Socioeconomic Level of Family	Language Background
A	5.2	99	Upper-lower	Monolingual
B	5.4	100	Upper-lower	Bilingual
C	5.6	96	Upper-lower	Bilingual

School records indicated that Subject A and Subject C were given the *Stanford–Binet Intelligence Scale* (Form M) in grade three, by a school psychometrist. At that time, Subject A's IQ was still 99, and Subject C's was 92.

Gains in Reading

Another way to examine reading progress is to look at gains in achievement level. The gains made by these 49 early readers, and their relation to intelligence, are summarized below:

Gains in Reading Grade-Level between September, 1958 and May, 1963		Correlation between Gains and Intelligence
RANGE	MEDIAN	
2.2—9.4	5.7	.67

To calculate the gains in reading achievement, each subject's grade-level score at the beginning of grade one was subtracted from his grade-level score at the conclusion of five years of school.[2] For these calculations, May, 1963, rather than May, 1964, was used as the terminal

[2] In calculating gains in achievement, it is recognized that a grade scale is not an equal-interval scale.

date because 1963 was the last year in which all 49 subjects were included in the testing.

As the data above show, the smallest individual gain in reading achievement over a five-year period was 2.2 years. This gain describes the progress of an early reader with an IQ of 91 who entered first grade reading at grade level 2.9, and who achieved a grade-level score of 5.1 at the end of fifth grade.

The greatest individual gain in achievement was 9.4 years. This gain is the progress of a subject with an IQ of 149 who started first grade with a reading grade-level score of 2.0 and who ended the fifth grade with a grade-level score of 11.4.

Test Results by Sex

Because sex differences in reading achievement are so very common, the next table, Table 3, repeats the data already summarized in Table 1, but organizes them according to sex. What stands out in this organization is that the relationship between achievement and intelligence became more pronounced for the girls than for the boys, as the years passed.[3]

Table 3. Reading progress of male and female subjects over a six-year period, and the relationship between progress and intelligence

| Date of Testing | Reading Grade-Level: | | | | Correlation between Reading Achievement and Intelligence | |
| | Range | | Median | | | |
	BOYS	GIRLS	BOYS	GIRLS	BOYS	GIRLS
Sept. 1958 (N=49)	1.5— 4.1	1.5— 4.6	2.1	1.9	.49	.35
May 1959 (N=49)	2.3— 5.2	2.6— 5.8	3.8	3.5	.75	.72
Sept. 1959 (N=49)	2.3— 5.6	2.4— 7.1	4.6	3.7	.78	.73
May 1960 (N=49)	3.8— 7.1	3.9— 8.9	5.0	4.9	.81	.80
May 1961 (N=49)	4.4— 8.6	4.6—10.6	5.8	5.2	.58	.78
May 1962 (N=49)	4.8—10.9	4.8—11.2	6.5	6.9	.54	.72
May 1963 (N=49)	5.0—10.8	5.1—11.7	7.3	7.6	.67	.86
May 1964 (N=34) [a]	5.4—11.2	5.2—12.3	7.9	9.6	.68	.72

[a] Because 15 of the original subjects had been double-promoted, only 34 were still in elementary school in the last year of the study.

[3] In examining a table like Table 3, it must be remembered that the size of a correlation coefficient is affected by the range of scores in each of the two variables.

Actually, though, this kind of sex difference is more striking in Table 4, which summarizes fifth-year data for the non-double-promoted subjects (the 34 subjects who were in grade five during the fifth year of the research). The next table, Table 5, singles out the 15 subjects who were double-promoted in the course of the research and were therefore in grade six during the fifth year of the study.[4] The table summarizes the reading achievement of these double-promoted children, and also shows a very marked relationship—in this instance, for both boys and girls— between achievement and intelligence.

Table 4. Reading achievement of the non-double-promoted subjects at the close of the fifth year of the research, and the relationship between achievement and intelligence

Subjects	Intelligence Quotient		Reading Grade-Level		Correlation: Reading Achievement and IQ
	MEDIAN	RANGE	MEDIAN	RANGE	
Boys and girls (N=34)	112	91—161	7.2	5.0—11.4	.72
Boys (N=12)	109	96—141	6.8	5.0—10.8	.48
Girls (N=22)	113	91—161	7.5	5.1—11.4	.82

Table 5. Reading achievement of the double-promoted subjects at the close of the fifth year of the research, and the relationship between achievement and intelligence

Subjects	Intelligence Quotient		Reading Grade-Level		Correlation: Reading Achievement and IQ
	MEDIAN	RANGE	MEDIAN	RANGE	
Boys and girls (N=15)	135	106—160	9.3	5.5—11.7	.84
Boys (N=8)	132	111—151	9.1	5.5—10.7	.84
Girls (N=7)	151	106—160	10.7	5.9—11.7	.86

[4] All of the intelligence and reading achievement data collected for the research were sent to schools attended by the subjects. However, this researcher deliberately refrained from making recommendations either about double promotions or about instructional programs for the early readers.

Comparison of Test Results for Double-Promoted and Non-Double-Promoted Early Readers

A comparison of the data in Table 4 with those in Table 5 reveals some differences between the double-promoted subjects and those who were not double-promoted. For instance, a comparison quickly indicates that it was the brighter children who generally were accelerated. This means, in turn, that Tables 4 and 5 are contrasting the achievement of double-promoted and non-double-promoted subjects, but also the achievement of bright subjects with that of the less bright ones.

The data in Tables 4 and 5 also show that it was the boys in particular who appeared to have profited from double promotion—at least in the sense that the achievement of double-promoted boys, in contrast to the achievement of the boys who were not double-promoted, more closely reflects their intelligence. Although this difference could be a chance effect, it is interesting to speculate about other factors that might account for it.[5]

Since 12 of the 15 double promotions in the California study took place during the first year, one possible explanation for the very close relationship between the achievement and the intelligence of the double-promoted boys lies in the extra challenge that resulted from their advancement into a higher grade. Such an explanation is plausible if two assumptions are valid: (1) that a typical second-grade reading program, as contrasted with a typical first-grade program, is more likely to offer instruction that is appropriately challenging for bright six-year-olds who have already begun to read; and (2) that boys, more than girls, profit from the challenge. Actually, the first of these assumptions was suggested by comments of the parents who, while being interviewed for the research, asked the interviewer why first-grade teachers were using pre-primers with their children even though the children could read more advanced material before they started school.

This question of the possibility of inappropriate school instruction, of course, raises another question about the possibility of arriving at reliable predictions about the future achievement of preschool readers. If a child who has learned to read early is treated in first grade as if he cannot read, it is clearly impossible to make an accurate assessment of the effect of his preschool learning on his subsequent achievement. Plans for this research did not include attempts to evaluate the degree to which school instruction for the 49 subjects corresponded to the level of their preschool achievement in reading. Consequently, all that can be done in this report is to describe the progress of the subjects as they moved from one grade to another in a variety of schools.

[5] Without knowledge either of the reasons why some early readers were accelerated or of the quality of instruction offered to all of them, comments about differences among correlation coefficients in Tables 4 and 5 cannot rise above the level of speculation.

Early Readers' Progress Related
to Characteristics of the Preschool Learning

The subjects' progress in reading—in this instance, as the progress relates to certain characteristics of the preschool learning—is shown in Tables 6 and 7. For both tables, information about the preschool learning was obtained in family interviews.[6] A word of explanation for the different variables shown in Tables 6 and 7 is in order before comments are made about the data themselves.

When families of the early readers were interviewed, it became clear that none of the subjects learned to read early "all by himself." What also became apparent was the wonderful productivity of a young child's questions—when they get answers—and, too, the large amount of achievement that can result from a small amount of informal help at home.

Some of the characteristics of this help are shown in Tables 6 and 7. In these tables the category *Age Started* indicates the age of the subject when help with reading was initiated at home. For the next category, that of *Frequency*, decisions in classifying parents' descriptions were affected both by the frequency and the regularity of the help. For instance, frequency described by such comments as "After he watched the television nursery school program in the morning," or "Generally a little everyday," or "When the other children were doing their homework in the evening" was classified as being *Often and regular*. Frequency explained by comments like "About a couple of times a week," or "We'd go to the library every two weeks, and I'd help her with the new books when we got home," or "Her sister played school with her practically every weekend," put this help under the classification *Less often and regular*. The classification *Intermittent* was for help described by such comments as "It seemed to go in spurts. Probably most of the help was given on rainy days or when it was too chilly to be outdoors, but even then it varied," or "Not too often. Only when she'd ask questions," or "I guess when she was interested and I was in the mood."

The next category, that of *Intent*, shows whether or not the help given at home was described as a deliberate attempt to teach a preschool child to read. As Table 6 indicates, 11 of the 49 subjects were reported to have received help from someone who was motivated by a conscious desire to teach reading.

The last characteristic, categorized as *Source*, has to do with the people in a young child's life who gave him some help with reading. Here, the classification *Combination* refers to help which came not only from parents and siblings, but also from other relatives and even neighbors.

In examining the data presented in Tables 6 and 7, it is especially important to keep in mind the very pronounced relationship—particularly

[6] A detailed report of the data obtained in family interviews appears in Chapter IV.

Table 6. Reading progress of the 49 early readers, over a five-year period, as related to various factors in the preschool learning

Preschool Help	Number of Subjects	Intelligence Quotient		Reading Grade-Level: Median						
		RANGE	MEDIAN	SEPT. 1958	MAY 1959	SEPT. 1959	MAY 1960	MAY 1961	MAY 1962	MAY 1963
Age started										
3 years	13	91—160	128.0	2.6	4.3	4.7	5.3	6.3	7.4	9.2
4 years	22	99—161	111.5	1.8	3.5	3.6	4.9	5.2	6.0	6.6
5 years	14	93—151	127.0	1.7	3.1	3.5	4.8	5.4	6.9	7.6
Frequency										
Often and regular	21	91—159	119.0	2.5	3.8	4.1	4.9	5.2	6.1	7.4
Less often and regular	21	93—151	112.0	1.8	3.5	3.6	4.7	5.2	6.7	7.2
Intermittent	7	99—161	132.0	1.6	3.7	4.0	5.4	5.9	7.6	9.8
Intent										
Deliberate	11	91—151	114.3	2.4	3.5	3.4	4.5	5.1	5.3	7.2
Not deliberate	38	93—161	123.5	1.9	3.7	4.1	4.9	5.5	6.9	7.9
Source										
Parent only	21	91—160	112.0	2.6	3.9	4.3	5.1	5.2	7.0	7.0
Sibling only	4	93—159	123.5	2.4	3.8	4.4	5.8	6.8	7.6	9.2
Combination of people	24	96—161	124.5	1.7	3.3	3.8	4.8	5.4	6.7	7.7

Table 7. Reading achievement of non-double-promoted subjects
in the sixth year of the research, as related to
various factors in the preschool learning

Preschool Help	Number of Subjects	Intelligence Quotient RANGE	MEDIAN	Reading Grade-Level: May, 1964 RANGE	MEDIAN
Age started					
3 years	6	91—141	128	7.9—11.1	9.9
4 years	17	99—161	109	5.2—11.8	8.4
5 years	11	93—149	119	5.4—12.3	9.8
Frequency					
Often and regular	14	91—149	114	5.4—12.3	8.8
Less often and regular	16	93—133	109	5.2—10.6	8.8
Intermittent	4	99—161	128	7.0—11.8	10.0
Intent					
Deliberate	10	91—149	114	5.6—12.3	8.8
Not deliberate	24	93—161	110.5	5.2—11.8	9.0
Source					
Parent only	13	91—149	108	5.6—12.3	8.1
Sibling only	2	93—112	102.5	8.0— 9.8	8.9
Combination of people	19	96—161	121	5.2—11.8	9.6

toward the end of the study—between reading achievement and intelligence. The close relationship means that intelligence accounted for a large percentage of the variance in reading achievement at the end of the research. It is assumed that the remaining variance is related to a number of variables, and that these might include the characteristics of the preschool learning which are enumerated in Tables 6 and 7.

Age and Readiness for Reading

Because so much of the professional literature concerned with reading readiness has concentrated on the age of a child when reading instruction begins, the only comments about readiness here, in connection with Tables 6 and 7, will focus on those data which show the chronological age at which the subjects initially received home help with reading and on those data concerned with intelligence. These two kinds of data are also presented in Table 8, with certain modifications. Added to them in Table 8 are estimated data about the mental age of the subjects when home help with reading began. The mental age data were calculated by using obtained data on chronological age and intelligence quotient.

More specifically, in preparing data for Table 8 the assumption was made that the 13 subjects reported to have received their first home help

Table 8. Reading progress of the 49 early readers over five school years, as related to chronological age, mental age, and intelligence quotient when home help with reading began

Chronological Age in Years	Mental Age in Years		Intelligence Quotient		Reading Grade-Level: Median	
	MEDIAN	RANGE	MEDIAN	RANGE	SEPT. 1958	MAY 1963
3.5 (N=13)	4.5	3.2—5.6	128.0	91—160	2.6	9.2
4.5 (N=22)	5.0	4.5—7.2	111.5	99—161	1.8	6.6
5.5 (N=14)	7.0	5.1—8.3	127.0	93—151	1.7	7.6

with reading at the chronological age of three (Table 6) received this help at ages that ranged from 3.0 years to 3.9 years.[7] Consequently, for Table 8, 3.5 was used to represent the chronological age, in years, at which each of these 13 subjects began to get help at home.

It was also assumed, in calculating the data for Table 8, that the first-grade intelligence quotients obtained in this research approximated the quotients that would have described the intelligence of the 13 subjects when their chronological age was 3.5 years [11]. Then, using the usual formula ($IQ = 100 \times MA/CA$), an approximate mental age was calculated for each of the 13 subjects as a way of describing the mental ability of each when home help with reading began. The median mental age for the group of 13, and the range of individual mental ages, are shown in Table 8.

Similar calculations, based on the same assumptions and the same reasoning, were made for the 22 subjects who first got help at the age of four, and for the 14 subjects who first got some help at the age of five. These results also are presented in Table 8.

In examining the data in Table 8, it is important to remember the very pronounced relationship between a subject's reading achievement and his intelligence, at the conclusion of five years of school (see Table 1). With this in mind, it is then meaningful to compare the reading achievement of the 13 subjects who first got help at home at a chronological age of about 3.5 years (median IQ = 128) with that of the 14 subjects who first received help at a chronological age of about 5.5 years (median IQ = 127). As Table 8 shows, the children who started to read at an earlier age entered first grade with superior achievement in reading; and they also maintained their lead over a five-year period. Such progress hardly supports the numerous proclamations of those who over the years have strongly discouraged pre-first-grade help with reading for all children.

[7] When parents were asked about the age at which their children first received help with reading, they were unable to be any more specific than "I think it must have been about three," or "I don't remember exactly, but probably about three."

Some Additional Comments about
the Early Readers' Progress

This first study of early readers was begun in an educational era whose spokesmen would promise little more than problems for children who received help with reading before the first grade. The problems were described differently at different times, but the descriptions generally included reference to (1) confusion when school instruction begins, and (2) an early loss of interest in reading. If "confusion" and "loss of interest" result in low achievement, then at least it can be conjectured that the early readers in this particular research had neither of these two problems to such an extent that it interfered with their progress in reading. As measured in the research, their progress can be described only in positive terms. Moreover, it must be remembered that the cause of such a problem as loss of interest could be related as much to an inappropriate first-grade reading program as to the early reading itself.

Of course, none of these comments presupposes that the methods used in this research to measure progress in reading were flawless. An objection might be made, for instance, to the use of different combinations of tests for different children at most of the testing periods. If this is a serious flaw, it could have been remedied only by having available a single test which was so comprehensive and so varied in difficulty that it could measure, equally well, vastly different achievement levels. As far as this writer knows, no such single test is on the market.

A testing problem of greater concern to the writer is the degree to which available reading tests seem to alter what they are measuring, as they become more difficult. For example, examination of the content of the various tests used in this research suggests that as the tests become increasingly more advanced, they also tend (1) to be more middle-class-oriented in their vocabulary items, and (2) to be related as much to reasoning ability as to reading ability in the tasks they require for successful performance. If this is true, it is especially noteworthy for interpreting this research report, inasmuch as 27 of the 49 subjects came from families below the middle-class level, and 17 subjects had IQ's of 109 or less.

Another Way of Studying the
Effect of Early Reading

To study the effect of early reading on subsequent achievement was one central purpose of this research. Such study has been carried on in two ways. The first procedure involved systematic testing of pre-first-grade readers over a six-year period in order to follow their reading progress throughout that period and, in particular, to see whether they would encounter problems when school instruction began. Data from this testing have been reported and discussed.

The second procedure for examining the effect of early reading developed out of a concern for the following question: What would be the achievement of the 49 subjects if they had not been early readers? Efforts to answer this question were to take the form of a periodic comparison of the reading achievement of the subjects, with the achievement of equally bright classmates who did not read before the first grade. Originally, the plan was to make the comparisons at the end of the third and sixth years of the research. However, because 15 subjects were double-promoted, a comparison was also made at the end of the fifth year, when these 15 children were getting ready to enter junior high school. A description of all the comparisons is given in subsequent sections of this chapter.

General Plans for Comparing Achievement

Periodic comparisons of the reading achievement of the early readers (experimental group) with the achievement of their classmates (control group) would be meaningful only if the factor of intelligence was taken into account. Consequently, research procedures included the collection of intelligence and reading achievement data for both groups.

While it would have been ideal to have Stanford–Binet intelligence data for both groups of children, the size of the expected control groups made the use of the Stanford–Binet scale impossible for these comparisons. As a result, the decision was to use intelligence data collected by the Oakland school system, for both the early readers and the control group. In the first of the comparisons of achievement, these intelligence data were to come from the *Kuhlmann–Anderson Mental Test*, Form B, administered each year to second-grade children. For the later comparisons, intelligence data were to come from the *Kuhlmann–Anderson Mental Test*, Form EF, administered each year to sixth-grade children [60].

Reading achievement data for the comparisons were also to come from school-administered tests. Here, too, it would have been more ideal to use with the control group the same testing procedures that were used with all of the early readers. However, the size of the expected control groups again made this kind of testing prohibitive. Consequently, the school reading data to be used for both groups were to come from the *Stanford Primary Reading Test*, Form J, administered each year to third-grade children, and, in later comparisons, from the *Stanford Intermediate Reading Test*, Form JM, administered each year to sixth-grade children [58].

All of the comparisons of achievement were designed to make a statistical judgment about the presence or absence of differences in the average reading achievement of equally bright early readers and non-early-readers, at the third-grade and sixth-grade levels. To make the judgment, the following procedures would be used.

In each of the comparisons of achievement, intelligence and reading achievement data for the control group (non-early-readers) would be used to calculate a regression equation for predicting reading achievement on the basis of intelligence. With this equation, predicted reading scores for each of the early readers would be calculated. These predicted scores then would be compared with the reading scores actually achieved by the early readers. Comparisons of actual and predicted scores would result in deviation scores. Then, to make a statistical evaluation of the observed differences, a t test of the null hypothesis would be carried out. Since a logical alternative to the null hypothesis was that the average achievement of the early readers would continue to be higher than that of non-early-readers, one-tailed t tests were used in all of the analyses. If the value of t was significant at the .05 level, the null hypothesis would be rejected.

Third-Year Comparison

The problems that developed in the third-year comparison clearly demonstrate some of the reasons for compromise and change in carrying out research plans. To be given here is a description both of what was planned and of what was actually done in the third-year comparison.

For this comparison, the intent was to include the 49 early readers (experimental group) and all the Oakland third-grade children who had not qualified as early readers but who had the same teachers as the early readers for the first three grades (control group). However, when the time came for the third-year comparison, 24 of the 49 early readers either had transferred to other school systems or had been double-promoted. This reduced the available experimental group to 25.

As it happened, the size of the expected control group was reduced too. This reduction was necessitated by problems connected with the school-administered intelligence test. Originally, all the intelligence quotients for the experimental and control groups in the third-year comparison were to have been derived from the *Kuhlmann–Anderson Mental Test,* Form B, administered by the Oakland school system during the second month of the second grade. However, examination of school records indicated that 4 of the 25 early readers who still were in Oakland third-grade classrooms had not taken this test. For the 21 early readers who had, the Kuhlmann–Anderson IQ's consistently underestimated the intelligence of the brighter children as it had been measured with the Stanford–Binet scale. Consequently, a decision was made to use the Stanford–Binet data already collected for the early readers, and to include in the control group only those third-grade children who had been given the *Revised Stanford–Binet Intelligence Scale* by the school system. Oakland schools use the Stanford–Binet scale more often than any other school system known to this writer; as a result, the control group numbered 201 children.

To describe reading achievement in the third-year comparison, the original plan was to use raw scores achieved on the *Stanford Primary Reading Tests,* Form J, administered by the school system in the seventh month of the third grade. Raw scores were selected in preference to their grade-level equivalents because, in the Stanford reading test to be used, grade equivalents for raw scores in the upper range of possible scores are assigned "by a process of extrapolation and cannot be interpreted as signifying the performance typical of pupils of the indicated grade placement" [58].

Later, when school records were examined, it was found that three schools—which included 5 of the 25 early readers still in Oakland—had not given the Stanford test. In its place, these schools had administered the *Gates Advanced Primary Reading Tests* (Form 2): *Word Recognition* and *Paragraph Reading*. In order to include in the experimental group the 5 early readers who had been given these Gates tests, grade-level scores rather than raw scores were used for both Stanford and Gates tests to describe reading achievement in the third-year comparison.

Results of the testing in reading are summarized in Table 9. Intelligence data also are given in Table 9.

Table 9. Reading achievement and intelligence data
in third-year comparison

Subjects	Reading Grade-Levels		Stanford–Binet IQ	
	RANGE	MEDIAN	RANGE	MEDIAN
Early readers (N=25)	4.4—6.0	5.0	91—161	114.8
Non-early-readers (N=201)	2.0—6.0	4.3	70—191	110.2

Having decribed some of the problems connected with the third-year comparison, it is now time to ask: How did the achievement of 25 of the early readers compare with the achievement of equally bright classmates who did not read early? To begin to answer this question, a scatter diagram was prepared in which a reading grade level and an intelligence quotient were plotted for each child in the experimental and control groups. What the diagram quickly revealed was the inadequacy of the school-administered reading test in establishing upper limits of achievement for the brighter children in both groups. More specifically, for children with IQ's above 120, the school-administered test was not sufficiently difficult, resulting in a ceiling and a very narrow range of reading scores. Consequently, a twofold comparison was planned between the achievement of the early readers and the achievement of the non-early-readers. The first comparison would focus on children with IQ's of 120 or less, the second on those with IQ's of 121 or higher.

Of the 201 children in the control group, 129 had IQ's of 120 or less. A first step in examining the value of a head start in reading was to calculate the coefficient of correlation between the intelligence and the reading achievement of these 129 children who were not early readers. This was found to be .61.

Next, the regression equation for predicting reading achievement on the basis of intelligence was formulated. The equation was then used to calculate predicted reading grade levels for each of the 15 early readers who also had IQ's of 120 or less. A comparison of predicted and obtained grade-level scores showed that all of these 15 early readers achieved at a higher level than would have been predicted on the basis of their intelligence. To see whether the deviation scores were significantly different from zero, a t test was performed. The obtained value of t ($t = 8.5$) was significant beyond the .0005 level.

For these 15 early readers with IQ's of 120 or less, individual deviations ranged from +0.2 years of achievement, to +1.3 years. The mean deviation was +0.7 years. That the quantitative advantage of an early start in reading appeared to be inversely related to the early reader's intelligence is shown in Table 10.

Table 10. Deviation of reading achievement of 15 early readers from expected achievement on the basis of intelligence

Intelligence Quotient: Range	Number of Early Readers	Mean Deviation in Years
91—100	5	+0.92
101—110	6	+0.68
111—120	4	+0.35

Now, what can be said about the value of a head start in reading for the other early readers still in Oakland schools—the 10 early readers who had IQ's higher than 120? In this third-year comparison, nothing. Because of the inadequacy of the school-administered reading test in identifying achievement levels for brighter children, the relationship between the intelligence and the reading achievement of the 72 non-early-readers with IQ's above 120, described by a correlation coefficient, was .17. With such a low correlation it did not make sense to calculate predicted reading scores for the 10 early readers on the basis of the relationship between intelligence and achievement in the control group. The hope was that more valid data would be available for the comparisons of achievement to be made in later years.

Fifth-Year Comparison

During the fifth year of the research, 15 early readers were in grade six because of double promotions. Of these, 12 were still attending Oakland public schools. Consequently these 12 children, equally divided between boys and girls, constituted the experimental group in the fifth-year comparison of the reading achievement of early readers and non-early-readers. The group of 12 attended nine schools, and were enrolled in nine different sixth-grade classrooms. Four of the nine classrooms were for "intellectually gifted children."

Original plans for the achievement comparisons included the decision to consider for control groups only those children who, over the years, had the same teachers as the early readers. However, because the early readers in this fifth-year comparison had been double-promoted, other selection criteria were established: the control group included all the children who were in the same sixth-grade classrooms as the 12 early readers, who had attended Oakland public schools in grades one through six, and who had been neither double-promoted nor retained in a grade for more than one year. With these selection criteria, then, the control group for the fifth-year comparison numbered 241 children—113 boys and 128 girls.

Whether any of these 241 sixth-graders were preschool readers was an unanswered question because, of course, they were in second grade at the time subjects for the research were identified. For purposes of the achievement comparison, they were considered to be non-early-readers.

In this fifth-year comparison, reading achievement data for both the experimental and the control groups came from the *Stanford Intermediate Reading Test*, Form JM, administered by the Oakland school system in February of the year of the comparison. The highest possible raw score on this test is 96; it was achieved by one early reader. Achieved scores for all of the early readers, and also for the non-early-readers, are summarized in Table 11.

Table 11. Reading achievement and mental age data
in fifth-year comparison

Subjects	Stanford Reading Test Raw Scores		Kuhlmann–Anderson Mental Age, in Years	
	RANGE	MEDIAN	RANGE	MEDIAN
Early readers (N=12)	61—96	87.5	10.9—17.2	14.0
Non-early-readers (N=241)	15—95	75.0	8.4—18.3	12.8

Intelligence data for the experimental and control groups came from the *Kuhlmann–Anderson Mental Test*, Form EF, also administered by the Oakland school system in February of the year of the comparison. Because, in this fifth-year comparison, the chronological age of the experimental group averaged one year less than the chronological age of the control group, mental age rather than intelligence quotient was used to describe the intelligence test results for both the experimental and the control groups. Mental age data are summarized in Table 11.

To make a comparison between the achievement of the double-promoted early readers and the achievement of the non-early-readers, a regression equation again was developed by using the reading achievement data and the mental age data for the group of 241 non-early-readers. For this group, the coefficient of correlation for achievement and mental age was .76.

With the regression equation, predicted reading scores for the 12 double-promoted early readers were calculated on the basis of their mental ages. The predicted raw scores then were compared with obtained raw scores, resulting in a deviation score for each early reader. In range, these deviation scores varied from −6.8 to +21.7. The mean deviation was +8.1. To see whether the deviation scores were significantly different from zero, a one-tailed t test was done. The obtained value of $t(t = 2.9)$ was significant at the .01 level. In terms of the hypothesis being tested, these findings indicated that double-promoted early readers, after five years of school instruction, show significantly higher levels of reading achievement than classmates (assumed to be non-early-readers) who were of the same mental age and had had six years of school instruction.

Table 12. Deviation of reading achievement of 12 double-promoted early readers from expected achievement on the basis of mental age

Mental Age in Years: Range	Number of Early Readers	Mean Deviation of Raw Scores
10.9—12.9	4	+12.5
13.0—15.0	5	+ 8.5
15.1—17.2 [a]	3	+ 1.2

[a] This range was increased by one-tenth of a year to include one subject who had a mental age of 17.2 years.

A way of looking at the magnitude of deviation scores, as it relates to mental age, appears in Table 12. Like the earlier data in Table 10, these data also suggest an inverse association between the intelligence of an early reader, and the quantitative advantage of his head start in reading.

Sixth-Year Comparison

At the time of the sixth-year comparison, 34 of the original 49 early readers were sixth-graders. However, only 25 of the 34 still were attending Oakland public schools. These 25 children, constituting the experimental group for this comparison, attended 22 schools. They were enrolled in 23 sixth-grade classrooms, four of which were for "intellectually gifted children." The group of 25 early readers was comprised of 15 girls and 10 boys.

The control group for the sixth-year comparison was comprised of sixth-graders in the same 23 classrooms as the early readers.[8] They were children who had attended Oakland public schools in grades one through six, and who had been neither double-promoted nor retained in a grade for more than one year. These selection criteria insured that no member of the control group had been an early reader, as early reading ability was defined in this study. For the sixth-year comparison, the control group numbered 636 children—329 girls and 307 boys.

How the experimental and control groups compared in intelligence is shown in Table 13. The intelligence data were derived from the *Kuhlmann–Anderson Mental Test*, Form EF, administered by the Oakland school system in February of the year of this comparison.

Table 13. Intelligence and reading achievement data in sixth-year comparison

Subjects	Kuhlmann–Anderson IQ		Stanford Reading Test Raw Scores	
	RANGE	MEDIAN	RANGE	MEDIAN
Early-readers (N=25)	89—149	121	55—95	81
Non-early-readers (N=636)	71—158	104	14—95	67

Reading achievement data for the experimental and control groups also appear in Table 13. The reading data are from the *Stanford Intermediate Reading Test*, Form JM, administered by the schools in February of the sixth-year comparison. The highest possible raw score on this test is 96.

---

[8] The original plan to include in the control group only children who, over the years, had the same teachers as the early readers was abandoned because the use of this criterion would have reduced the control group to a negligible size.

In the control group, the correlation coefficient for reading achievement and intelligence was .76. Once again, the regression equation derived from these reading achievement and intelligence data was used to calculate predicted reading scores for the 25 early readers, on the basis of each early reader's IQ. A comparison of obtained and predicted raw scores was made. The deviation scores that resulted ranged from —15.0 to +21.3. The mean deviation was +2.9. When a one-tailed t test was carried out to see whether the deviation scores were significantly different from zero, the obtained value of t ($t = 1.6$) was not significant at the .05 level.[9]

Table 14. Deviation of reading achievement of 25 early readers from expected achievement on the basis of intelligence

Intelligence Quotient: Range	Number of Early Readers	Mean Deviation of Raw Scores
89—104	5	+6.3
105—120	7	+7.9
121—136	9	+1.8
137—152	4	—7.4

How, in this sixth-year comparison, an early reader's IQ was related to the difference between his obtained and predicted reading scores is shown in Table 14. Again, an inverse association exists between IQ and the magnitude of a deviation score, but the association is not as pronounced as in the third- and fifth-year comparisons.

Research Problems in the Achievement Comparisons

Before a synthesis of findings from the three achievement comparisons is made, problems connected with each of the comparisons ought to be made explicit. Otherwise the findings might gain an acceptance not merited by the nature or quality of the research from which they came.

One obvious problem in the third-year comparison of achievement was the inadequacy of the school-administered reading test for the brighter children. Its insufficient difficulty allowed only for a comparison of early and non-early-readers who had IQ's of 120 or less.

Another special problem in the third-year comparison relates to the use of Stanford–Binet intelligence data. For the control group in this comparison, the Stanford–Binet Scale had been administered by the

[9] A t value of 1.7 would be significant at the .05 level.

Oakland schools. Because public school systems often need to reserve the use of individual intelligence tests for children who are somewhat deviant either in behavior or academic achievement, or both, it is possible that the control group in the third-year comparison was not as typical a population as, for instance, the control groups in the fifth- and sixth-year comparisons.

In the fifth- and sixth-year comparisons, however, there were other shortcomings. For example, in the fifth-year comparison there was no way of knowing whether any of the 241 children in the control group had been preschool readers. Because these children were in grade two at the time subjects for this research were being identified, none was involved in the original screening process.

Another problem, one common to both the fifth- and the sixth-year comparisons, was the need to use data from a group intelligence test. Because high performance on group intelligence tests is so dependent upon high achievement in reading, the mental ages and the IQ scores derived from them are not always as valid as research requires.

In the fifth- and sixth-year comparisons, a question also needs to be raised about the adequacy of the one reading test for identifying levels of achievement for the brighter children. Scatter diagrams showed some restrictions placed by this test upon their performance, but not enough to warrant separate comparisons based on IQ levels.

Finally, a problem common to the fifth- and sixth-year comparisons, and also shared by the comparison done in the third year, was the small number of children in the experimental groups. The paucity of early readers, of course, is a problem for the whole of this first study. However, when a small group of 49 subjects diminishes still further—as happened in the achievement comparisons—then two different kinds of questions must be asked. If, as in the third- and fifth-year comparisons, early readers are achieving at significantly higher levels than equally bright non-early-readers, then a question must be raised about the general applicability of findings from such a small sample. On the other hand, when early readers do not show significantly higher achievement, as in the sixth-year comparison, then the appropriate question is whether the failure to find a significant difference is due to the small number of cases examined or to a true equality of the two groups.

Now, with this variety of questioning as a background, attention will be given to a summary of what was found in the three comparisons of reading achievement made in this first study.

Summary of Findings in the Achievement Comparisons

In each of these three comparisons, the intent of the research was to test the following null hypothesis: There is no significant difference between the average reading achievement of equally bright early readers and non-early-readers as they move through the elementary school years. The one-tailed t tests carried out in the third- and fifth-year comparisons showed average achievement differences to be positive—that is, in favor of the early readers—and also significantly different from zero at the .05 level. For each of these two comparisons, then, the null hypothesis stated above can be rejected.

The sixth-year comparison also showed higher average achievement for the early readers, but the differences were not significant at the .05 level. Consequently, in the sixth-year comparison the null hypothesis stated above cannot be rejected.[10]

A different kind of finding—one common to all three of the achievement comparisons—had to do with the inverse association between the intelligence level of the early reader and the quantitative advantage of his early start in reading. This kind of association suggested that an earlier beginning in reading might be of special value for the slower child. If true, why might this be so?

One plausible answer could be that bright children will do well in reading regardless of the age at which they begin to read. Such an answer, however, evades the more specific question of why the less bright children among the early readers seemed to be more successful in maintaining their lead over non-early-readers of comparable intelligence.

The hypothetical explanation offered by this researcher is that the earlier start in reading was of special value to the less bright children because it gave them a longer amount of time to make advancements in their achievement. With the additional time, more opportunities were available for repetition and for practice. While such repetition, with its slower pace, might be a source of boredom for the brighter child, the same repetition might be exactly what the less bright child needs in order to achieve at a maximum level.

Summary of Findings Using Combined Data

It will be recalled that the fifth-year comparison of achievement was required by the fact that some of the 49 early readers had been double-promoted, and so were in grade six during the fifth year of the study. It has also been mentioned that the average achievement of these double-promoted subjects was significantly higher than that of classmates with the same mental age, even though the early readers had had one year less of school instruction in reading.

To be recalled, too, is the fact that the double-promoted subjects tended to be the best readers among the total group of 49 early readers (see Tables 4 and 5). Consequently, when the double-promoted children

[10] It should be remembered that the fifth-year comparison involved early readers who had been double-promoted, and that the sixth-year comparison only involved early readers who had not been accelerated.

were not available for the sixth-year comparison, some of the most successful readers were being eliminated. It is therefore appropriate to
ask: If, for the sixth-year comparison, the experimental group were comprised both of the double-promoted and the non-double-promoted early
readers, how would the average achievement of this new experimental
group compare with the average achievement of the original sixth-year
control group?

To answer this question, the reading achievement data for the 12
double-promoted early readers (experimental group in fifth-year comparison) were combined with the reading achievement data for the 25
non-double-promoted early readers (experimental group in sixth-year
comparison). The combined data then were used to describe the achievement of a new experimental group of 37 children. The control group was
the 636 non-early-readers who constituted the control group for the sixth-
year comparison already described. Data from the *Stanford Intermediate
Reading Test*, Form JM, and data from the *Kuhlmann–Anderson Mental
Test*, Form EF, were again used for both groups of children. In this
particular analysis, mental age data rather than intelligence quotients
were used to describe groups because the 12 double-promoted early
readers were younger than the other children by approximately one year.
Raw scores again were used to describe reading achievement.

Using the regression equation derived from the mental age and
reading achievement data for the control group, predicted reading scores
were calculated for each of the 37 early readers on the basis of mental
age. Predicted scores and obtained scores then were compared. Results
showed individual deviation scores ranging from -13.8 to $+22.6$. The
mean deviation score was $+5.1$. When a one-tailed t test was done, the
obtained value of t ($t = 1.8$) was significant at the .05 level.

In terms of the null hypothesis being tested, these findings indicated
that the average achievement of early readers who had had either five
or six years of school instruction in reading, was significantly higher than
the average achievement of equally bright classmates who had had six
years of school instruction but were not early readers.

Chapter **IV**

Family Interviews
in the First Study

The writer's first formal contact with a preschool reader, described in Chapter I, provoked many questions about this particular kind of precociousness: How many children enter first grade already reading? Will most of these early readers be girls? Does early reading ability require a high level of intelligence? Do early readers most often come from middle- and upper-class families? Do early readers teach themselves to read, or do they have parents who carry on school-like instruction at home? Will early readers have problems with reading, once they enter first grade?

Answers to certain questions about preschool reading could come from tests; some answers of this kind have already been reported. Other questions, however, only could be answered by having information about the families of early readers. To collect the information, home interviews were held with the families of the 49 early readers in the research. All the interviewing was done by this writer during the year the children were in first grade.

Interviews as Sources of Data

Even if there had been an abundance of earlier studies of preschool reading from which the most relevant interview questions could have been identified, interview data in this present study would still be subject to certain "human errors." With the most perfect of interview questionnaires, for example, responses of an interviewee can be inaccurate because of such factors as confusion, forgetting, exaggeration, or even deliberate concealment. This is to say, simply, that what is described in this chapter is what parents were both able and willing to report in the home interviews.

Questionnaire for Home Interviews

The purpose of the interviews in this first study was to explore some of the family factors that might encourage preschool achievement in reading. Selection of questions for the interviews was guided by the researcher's special interest in the improvement of school efforts to teach beginning reading. The hope was that information about the ways children learn to read at home would suggest more effective ways for teaching reading in the schools. This "curriculum" emphasis, of course, implied no doubt about the relevance to early reading of "psychological" factors such as those relating to personality structures of family members or to sibling or parent–child relationships. In fact, it is likely that a complete assessment of the psychological dynamics in each subject's family would be the only way to arrive at explanations as well as descriptions of the preschool reading that is the focus of this research. Nonetheless, the general tone of the interview questionnaire was definitely not psychological.

Questions selected for the home interviews came from several sources.[1] Some were suggested in the informal interview that was held with the parents of Midge—the early reader who could be described as the "cause" of this research. Others came from subsequent conversations with about a dozen parents of preschool children. Still other questions were asked because they were so logically related to early reading ("Did you ever read to your child before he started kindergarten?").

Tentatively selected questions were tried out in interviews with acquaintances who were parents of preschool children. As a result of these practice sessions, the wording of some of the original questions was altered to clarify their meaning; and two new questions were added ("Do any adults live here, other than you and your husband?" and "Did any of your other children learn to read before they started first grade?").

The content of the final form of the questionnaire centered around three general topics: (1) family background; (2) the early reader; and (3) his early reading ability. Some of the interview questions were open-ended ("What do you have around the house that might encourage a young child's interest in reading?"). Others were more specifically structured ("Did you ever want to be a teacher?"). Some of the questions dealt with verifiable facts ("Did your child go to nursery school?"). Other questions also dealt with facts, but answers depended upon a retrospection that is not always infallible ("At what age did your child first show an interest in written words and numbers?"). Still other interview questions asked for opinions and judgments ("Do you think reading ought to be taught only by a trained person?").

In all of the questioning, a conscious effort was made by the interviewer to refrain from passing judgment—either by words or facial ex-

[1] A copy of the questionnaire can be found in Appendix B.

pressions—on a parent's response. A deliberate effort also was made to refrain from giving an opinion about the value or about the problems of preschool reading ability. This decision held even when parents directly asked for an opinion.

The Interviews

The first of the 49 interviews was done on October 7, 1958. The last was completed on December 5, 1958. In each case, this writer was the interviewer.

To insure that the early readers would not be at home, the plan was to do the interviewing on weekdays, between 9 A.M. and 3 P.M.[2] The selection of these hours, of course, reduced the number of interviews for which both the mother and father were available. In 11 instances, the two parents were able to be present. For 37 other interviews, however, only the mother was available either because the father was at work (32 cases) or because the parents were divorced (5 cases). For the remaining interview it was the early reader's grandmother who was available; in this instance the grandmother had raised the child because his mother was mentally ill and had been institutionalized since his birth.[3]

Interviewing time in this first study ranged from 60 minutes to 150 minutes, with an average length of 90 minutes. Essentially the same questions were asked in each interview, but interviewees varied in the time they took to respond.[4] The interviewer deliberately avoided rushing anybody. The end result was much information about preschool reading—and, in addition, much information about life in general. (In some interviews it was as if the parent had long been waiting to find an interested listener to talk to about her most pressing problems.)

At the request of the Oakland school system, parents of early readers were first contacted about the interviews by school principals. Once general permission was granted—and no parent refused—this writer made a second phone call to arrange for definite dates and times.

The reason given to parents for the interviews was the writer's interest in learning about the preschool years. Their children's early achievement in reading was cited as one of the reasons why they were selected. No parent asked about other possible reasons, but five stressed the minimal nature of the achievement.

At the start of an interview, the writer assured each parent that all information given would be held in strict confidence, and that none would be passed on to the school. To give added support to the promise of anonymity, no tape recorder was used. Instead, responses were written

[2] One interview was done on a Sunday afternoon because the mother, a divorcée, worked six days a week.

[3] In the report of interview data, this grandmother will be treated as the mother.

[4] Certain interview questions were not pertinent to all families. For example, questions about older siblings were not asked when a subject was an only child.

down by the interviewer as they were given by the parent.[5] Immediately
following an interview, the responses were typed by the interviewer on
a second but identical questionnaire form, simply to replace the original
"chicken scratching" with a record that was both legible and permanent.

Reporting of Interview Data

Once the 49 interviews were completed, analysis of the data they
yielded began. Although these data do not always fit neatly into distinct
categories, findings will nevertheless be reported under the three major
topics with which the questions dealt: (1) family background, (2) the
early readers, and (3) their early reading ability. Some commentary
will be interwoven with the findings—in a way, it is hoped, that will aid
interpretation without encouraging unfounded conclusions.

Family Backgrounds of the Early Readers

Before the subjects for this research were identified, it was assumed
that most early readers would come from families of professional status.
Such an expectation grew out of the educational literature, which often
points to success in reading as being associated with membership in the
higher socioeconomic classes [71, 81, 87]. However, few of the families
of these 49 subjects would be classified as professional. When interview
information on (1) father's occupation, (2) source of income, (3) house
type, and (4) dwelling area was appraised by means of Warner's "Index
of Social Class Scale" [98], only 7 of the families were identified as upper-
middle class. The distribution of the 49 families with respect to socioeconomic status was as follows:

	Number	Per cent
Upper-middle	7	14
Lower-middle	15	31
Upper-lower	26	53
Lower-lower	1	2

What this distribution shows is that families of the "blue-collar class"
predominated. Why?

One possible explanation might be a preponderance of children from
blue-collar families in the Oakland public schools, or at least in the first-
grade population from which early readers were identified. No conclusion
can be reached about this possibility—first, because the Oakland schools
had no socioeconomic data for their students, and, second, because this
researcher made no attempt to identify the socioeconomic backgrounds of
all the 5,103 children who were tested for early reading ability.

[5] In the 11 interviews for which both parents were present, there were no instances of overt contradiction in responses to questions. Actually, in 9 of these interviews, the mother tended to answer the questions while the father assumed the role
of listener; in the other 2 interviews, these roles were reversed.

Another possible explanation for the large number of early readers from blue-collar families might be that (as has been claimed [95]) Warner's Index underestimates the social class status of nonwhites. This possibility requires attention in this research report, inasmuch as 23 of the 49 subjects were either Negro (12) or Oriental (11). Of these 23 non-Caucasian children, 7 were categorized as lower-middle class, 15 as upper-lower class, and 1 as lower-lower class.

Still another possible reason for the large number of early readers from blue-collar families has two related components: (1) the family interviews were done in 1958, in an era when preschool reading was still strongly discouraged by the schools; and (2) professional-level parents, in contrast to parents of a lower socioeconomic status, would be more aware of official school policy regarding the early teaching of reading. Some verification of this reasoning is found in the following distribution of "Yes" and "No" responses to the interview question *Do you think reading ought to be taught only by a trained person?* [6]

	Yes	No
Upper-middle	7 (100%)	0
Lower-middle	6 (40%)	9 (60%)
Upper-lower	4 (15%)	22 (85%)
Lower-lower	0	1 (100%)

As the interviews progressed, it was not surprising to find that concern about the possible problems resulting from early reading was clearly visible in the 7 families of the upper-middle class. In all interviews with these families, the interviewer was asked whether reading problems really would develop as the children got older. In contrast, the attitude of the 27 families classified as upper-lower and lower-lower was one of optimism. In these families there was obvious pride in the early reading achievement of their children. It was as if early reading was just the beginning of better things to come.

In spite of these kinds of findings, however, there is no attempt in this report to suggest a simple one-to-one relationship between social class status and parental opinion about preschool reading. It certainly can be assumed, for example, that the presence of an early reader in any family might have some effect on that family's attitude toward preschool reading, regardless of social class status. That this was so is demonstrated in the explanation which one parent gave for her belief that the teaching of reading does not require a trained person:

> I used to think that special training was needed, but now I don't think so because D____ has done so well. I do feel, though, that parents should go according to some book or plan.

[6] Throughout the report of interview data, it is important to remember that some parents may have given what they considered to be "correct" responses.

That attitudes toward preschool reading can be affected by very individual family factors was especially emphasized in an interview with the mother of two children, the second of whom was the early reader. In this family, the older child was mentally retarded. As a result, the mother explained in the interview, she and her husband were so grateful to find their second child alert and curious that they "jumped for joy" whenever she asked a question about anything. For this family, then, a child's preschool interest in reading was "concrete proof that she was normal," and it seemed to have elicited an enthusiastic response from her parents.

What else did the research interviews reveal about families of early readers? In this particular study, interview data indicated that 10 of the 49 families were bilingual. In 7 of these, the second language was Chinese; in 2, it was Spanish; and in 1, German. In the case of the 7 Chinese bilingual families, 3 mothers were unable to read English.

As a group, however, the parents of the 49 subjects not only could read but did. When they were asked in the interviews whether they themselves read "more than the average adult," many responded affirmatively.[7] Below is a summary of responses to the questions *Do you read more than the average adult?* and *Does your husband read more than the average adult?*

	Number
Mother and father both read "more than the average"	6
Only the mother reads "more than the average"	14
Only the father reads "more than the average"	11
Neither mother nor father reads "more than the average"	18

Interview data concerned with family size showed the number of children in each of the 49 families ranged from one to eight, with a median of three children. There were 3 singletons among the subjects, and 6 others were the oldest of the children in their families. This left 40 subjects who had at least one older brother or sister, a fact that became very relevant as parents were queried about the ways their children learned to read early.

The Early Readers

According to family interview data, the 49 early readers in this study entered first grade at chronological ages that ranged from 5 years 9 months, to 6 years 9 months. The median age for the group was 6 years 4 months. The range in chronological age reflected the fact that the Oakland school system required a minimum age of 5 years 9 months for entrance into grade one and also adhered to an annual promotion system which allowed children to begin first grade only in the fall of the year.

[7] In the interview, the "average adult reader" was described as "one who reads newspapers, perhaps a magazine, and occasionally a book."

Interview data about the earlier years of the subjects showed that 10 had been to nursery school. These nursery school experiences varied, in duration, from six months to three years; and, in kind, from city-supported Child Care Centers to a private "Rhythm School" in which music history and music appreciation were the curriculum.

Of the 47 early readers who attended kindergarten, all went to Oakland public school kindergartens, and for one year. An early reader who did not go to kindergarten spent her fifth year in a Child Care Center which she had been attending since the age of three. In this case, the mother's need to work required all-day care for the child. Why another of the early readers did not get to kindergarten was explained by his father, who characterized kindergarten as "a year that spoiled my older son," as "a waste of time," and as "a place where they just let them play."

Other interview data concerned with the past history of the early readers revealed no illnesses that were unusual either in kind or in duration. To be sure, there were the normal childhood diseases; all of the children, for instance, had had measles and mumps.

Although factors like faulty memory and varied meanings for identical words raise some doubts—and rightly so—about the accuracy of answers to such questions as *At what age did your child begin to walk?* and *At what age did he begin to talk?* these two questions were nevertheless asked in the interviews.[8] Answers indicated that the subjects began to walk at ages ranging from 8 months to 18 months (mean, 12 months); and that talking began at ages that ranged from 8 months to 24 months (mean, 14 months). Actually, the mean age for each of these two kinds of development was not much below what has been cited for the "average child"—14 months for walking, and 15 months for talking [37, 63].

Of special relevance to this research was the age at which curiosity about written language was first shown by the subjects. According to interview data, the children began asking questions about written words and numbers at ages that varied from 2 years to 5 years (mean, 3 years); and they began to print words and numbers at ages ranging from 2 years to 6 years (mean, 4 years).[9]

To be noted, too, is the fact that 6 of the 49 subjects were left-handed and 43 were right-handed. None, according to parental observations, showed a tendency to be ambidextrous. None, either, was reported to have any observable vision problems.

In the interviews, parents were also asked about their observations regarding the personality characteristics of the early readers. Here, the interview question was really a series of questions, asked one after the

---

[8] The initial stage of walking was defined, in the interviews, as "the age at which a child could walk across a room without assistance." The initial stage of talking was defined as "the age at which a stranger would be able to understand what the child said."

[9] Without exception, parents gave the age for talking and walking in terms of months, but the age for beginning reading and printing in years.

other: *How would you describe your child in terms of his temperament and attitudes? For example, in what ways is he either like other children or different from them? What words would best describe him?* When a parent appeared to have finished responding to this series of questions, the interviewer then said: *I don't know your child. Are there any other words that would help me to know the kind of child he is?*

Although many descriptions of a child were given throughout an interview, only responses to the series of successive questions just presented will be used to portray the early readers, as seen by their parents. This decision was made because some parents gave information only in response to interview questions while others talked very freely, with and without the aid of questions. Such variability dictated the use of responses to questions which were asked of all parents.

In responding to the series of questions mentioned above, parents sometimes used synonymous terms to describe their children. For instance, in one of the interviews a parent described her son as "happy-go-lucky." Later on, in response to the same series of questions, she said, "Nothing ever seems to bother him." In such cases, the two (or more) responses were counted as denoting one and the same characteristic.

In other instances, however, it was not clearly apparent whether responses should be treated as synonymous. Is the description of a child as "competitive" equivalent to one which says, "He was always so eager to keep up with his older brother"? In cases where equivalence was not obvious and clear-cut, differently worded responses were classified as referring to different characteristics.

As given here, then, the characteristics of the early readers, as seen by their parents, are shown in a list of nonsynonymous descriptive terms. The number in parentheses after each term is the number of subjects described as having the given characteristic, whether in the same or equivalent terms.

Characteristics of Subjects As Seen by Parents

Persistent (35)	Bossy (4)
Perfectionistic (20)	Friendly (4)
High-strung (16)	Good sense of humor (4)
Good disposition (15)	Needs to be praised (4)
Serious (15)	Shy (4)
Neat (13)	Independent (3)
Worrier (11)	Intelligent (3)
Competitive (10)	Keeps things to himself (3)
Curious (10)	Moody (3)
Happy-go-lucky (9)	Affectionate (2)
Good memory (8)	Active (2)
Quiet (8)	Impatient (2)
Feelings easily hurt (8)	Ambitious (1)
Eager to keep up with older	Dependent (1)
sibling (7)	Eager to please adults (1)

It is important to remember the questions that could be raised about the value of these data as realistic descriptions of the subjects. For example, there must always be some doubt about the possibility of a parent being truly objective about his own child. In addition, it must be recognized that some parents are more adept than others at discerning the particular characteristics of a child, and also that some parents are better able to put their perceptions into words. Not to be forgotten, either, is the possibility that one parent might tend to overrate his child, while another might be too modest. In the case of the interviews for this study, there is also the need to remember that the reasons given for the interviewing, combined with the nature of the questions, might have encouraged exaggerated emphasis on certain phases of the subjects' preschool years.

Another point to bear in mind is the fact that the responses noted in this list of characteristics are those which were given for one particular series of interview questions. This is important because, in some interviews, characteristics like "persistent," "curious," and "has an excellent memory" were cited at various points in an interview, yet were not mentioned again when the parent was directly asked to characterize his child. One explanation—and if true it would limit the value of these data as characterizing this group of children—might be the parent's hesitancy to repeat a description given earlier. A second possible explanation could be that a tendency which might have been very influential in stimulating a child's desire to become a reader ("eager to keep up with her older sister," for example) was not felt to be a pervasive characteristic of the child.

Another question about the data on characteristics—and this was a question that constantly plagued this researcher—concerned the degree to which they describe early readers as contrasted with non-early-readers. Or, to put the query in another form: If parents of 49 non-early-readers were asked to describe their children, would the same characteristics be given, and with comparable frequency? This kind of wondering was one reason for the second study of early readers which is described in later chapters of this report.

For now, there is only one other kind of information to add about the early readers in the first study. The source of this information was the children themselves. Curious about their recollections of the time they first learned to read, this researcher spoke with the subjects when they were being tested in reading at the end of the first year of the study. Deliberately, these conversations were kept informal and unstructured. The only agenda strictly adhered to was the asking of three questions: (1) *When did you first learn to read?* (2) *Who was it who first taught you to read?* (3) *How did he/she/they teach you?* These questions were posed at any point in the conversations that made the questioning appear natural and spontaneous. To explain why the answers were being written, the children were told that writing answers makes it easier to remember them.[10]

When questioned about the time they first learned to read, 38 subjects showed awareness of having learned at home, and before entering first grade; 4 other subjects said they could not recall when they first learned; 7 said they began to read after they entered first grade.

Although only 38 of the subjects specifically mentioned having learned to read at home, 42 referred to people other than a teacher as having initially taught them.[11] Of these 42, 26 said a parent was their first teacher. Asked how the teaching had been done, the 26 children responded in a variety of ways, but the following explanations are representative:

> She [mother] told me the words. Then I started to read, and when I'd forget she'd tell me.
>
> She showed me the words and told me what they said. I wanted to go to school, and they wouldn't take me until I was old enough.
>
> I started writing words, and then I learned how to read.
>
> He'd [father] read a bunch of books, and he wanted us to read. My mother helped me.
>
> She taught me how to sound out the words.

Among the group of 14 subjects who said older siblings had first taught them to read, the following accounts of the teaching are both typical and interesting:

> She [sister] was the best reader in the class. She got books for me. She told me what the words said.
>
> She brought home papers with lots of words. She studied and she kept on telling me the words.
>
> She read a book to me, and she pointed them [words] out when she said them.
>
> When my sister's not too busy she tells me words.
>
> My sister taught me how to sound out words. Now she doesn't play school so much because I know a lot of things.
>
> He [brother] told me every word in each book. He said, "Write these and you'll remember them."

One other subject said she taught herself to read "by sounding out the words." Still another gave most of the credit for her early reading to a friend:

---

[10] Three subjects recalled their teachers' saying it was easier to remember how to spell a new word if the word was written.

[11] Interview data about the persons who helped the children are given on page 53.

Tom M_____ first taught me. He's about nine. I played with him. He told me that "look" has two eyes, and that "see" has two "e's." He showed me words and stuff. Then I came home. My brother was reading and I wanted to read too. I'd ask my mother. She was surprised I could read.

The Early Reading Ability

Descriptions by subjects of the ways they first learned to read provide a natural introduction to what was reported in/the family interviews; for, from the two sources, descriptions tended to be similar. This is not to say, however, that the 49 reports of preschool reading ability given by parents were identical. While there were many responses and explanations that were repeated from one interview to another, the response data from the 49 interviews did not add up to 49 identical information patterns. Lacking one single pattern, interview data about the ways subjects learned to read early will be presented in this report in the form of answers to questions focusing on (1) the most influential person in the early learning, (2) the kinds of help given to the early readers, and (3) the factors that motivated the help.

Who was the most influential person in the early learning?

There were 3 singletons among the subjects in this study, and 6 subjects were the oldest of the children in their families. For this group of 9, the mother was the one who provided direct help in their early acquisition of reading ability.[12]

Of the 40 subjects who had at least one older brother or sister, 16 were given direct help by one person while the other 24 received direct help from a combination of people. These sources and the number of interviews in which each was mentioned for this group of 40 can be summarized as follows:

One person (N = 16)		*Combination (N = 24)*	
Mother	10	Mother, sister	12
Father	2	Mother, brother	4
Sister	2	Father, sister	3
Brother	2	Father, brother	2
		Mother, brother, aunt	1
		Mother, grandmother	1
		Mother, peer	1

[12] In this study *direct help* refers to word identification and to the giving of information about the sounds of letters. When "playing school" included either of these kinds of help, it was also classified as direct. *Indirect help* was more varied and ranged from help with spelling to the purchase of materials which could assist a child in learning to read.

What kinds of help were given to the early readers?

As has been indicated, the one source of direct help with preschool reading for 21 subjects was a parent; for 24 other subjects, a parent was one of a combination of people who helped. The kinds of direct help given by these parents, and the number of interviews in which each kind of help was mentioned, are shown below:

Talked about sounds of letters	29
Identified words for subjects	14
Played school with subjects	2

Parental help considered to be indirect was more varied, and was mentioned with greater frequency:

Read to subject	49 [13]
Bought alphabet book, or picture dictionary, or both	38
Helped subject with printing	37
Helped older sibling with reading while subject watched	25
Bought easy basal readers	20
Bought school-like reading workbook	18
Helped subject with spelling	18
Helped subject with word meanings	7
Helped subject find material in encyclopedia	3

Four subjects in this study received direct help with reading only from an older sibling. However, sibling help was part of a combination of sources of direct help for 22 other subjects. How all of these siblings gave direct help with reading is described below:

Played school with subject	16
Identified words for subject	16
Talked about sounds of letters	8

Sibling help of a more indirect kind, and the number of interviews in which each kind was mentioned, can be described as follows:

Read to subject	35
Helped subject with printing	14
Helped subject with spelling	5
Helped subject find material in encyclopedia	1

[13] Four subjects received no direct help with reading from their parents. However, all 49 of the early readers had been read to by one or both parents before they were old enough for school.

What motivated the preschool help with reading?

That all of the subjects in this first study were given some kind of help with reading became apparent in the course of the family interviews. What also became clear was the multiplicity of factors that encouraged this preschool help. For instance, 11 parents said they deliberately set out to teach their preschool children to read. Yet, even among these parents, different factors prompted their decision. Five mothers in the group said their children were so persistently interested in learning to read that they decided to teach them. One father in a bilingual family explained that his oldest daughter had difficulty learning to read, and had to repeat first grade; consequently, when each of his other three children reached the age of about five, he started giving them help in reading to avoid future problems in school. One mother—and she was the only mother in the study who was a teacher—said her daughter was ready to learn to read when she was five, so she started giving the child help at home. The other 4 mothers in this group of 11 parents said they taught their children to read early because they felt it was their responsibility as parents to get them ready to do well in first grade. For them, this meant giving the child a head start in reading.

For all of the 38 subjects in this study who did not have someone in their family who deliberately planned to teach them to read early, preschool help was given primarily because of their overt curiosity about written words and numbers. The actual amount of help given in these cases, then, depended upon the frequency and the persistence of the children's questions—and upon the patience and free time of people in their families.[14]

Because of the obvious importance of curiosity and interest as factors in the early reading ability of the subjects in this study, efforts were made to identify the sources from which the children's preschool interest in reading developed. In the family interviews, the following sources were mentioned as being especially important, in the frequencies shown:

Being read to at home	44
Eagerness to keep up with older sibling	23
Availability of reading materials in the home	21
Availability of blackboard	19
Interest in learning to print	10
Curiosity about TV advertisements	8
Interest in how to spell words	6
Curiosity about outdoor signs	5
Desire to read correspondence from out-of-town relatives	3
Interest in the encyclopedia	1

[14] For detailed information about the frequency and regularity of the preschool help with reading, see Table 6 on page 27.

Impressions from the Interviews

Some comments have already been made about the data from family interviews in the first study; and others will be added when interview data from the second study are discussed. Now, the intent is to present what can only be called the general impressions of someone who had the opportunity to talk with many parents of young children. As reported here, the impressions are a kind of quick summary of the spontaneous and unstructured notes made by the writer following each of the 49 interviews.

One outstanding impression left by many of the interviews had to do with the uneasy concern of parents about their role as educators of the preschool child in matters like reading and writing. Especially in the middle-class families, there was an expression almost of guilt feelings as parents told about the ways their children learned to read. These parents also asked many questions about the warnings that had come from PTA meetings, from the teachers of older children in the family, and from newspaper and magazine articles telling parents that preschool reading would only lead to problems and confusion when school instruction began.

Although the writer of the letter presented below was not involved in either of these two studies of early reading, the content summarizes very accurately the concern shown in 1958 in some of the California interviews. The letter, written to this researcher by a parent in the Midwest, follows:

> My first child I completely discouraged from reading before he was taught in school. My second child learned to read while in kindergarten but the teacher informed me not to encourage it. Now my 4½ year old son has started reading. How he learned I'm not quite sure; one morning he was sitting there reading different words. I took the book later and sort of hid it. He found it again and, as you say, they are persistent.
>
> You hit the nail on the head when you said they are curious, persistent, and perfectionistic.[15] I had considered these bad personality characteristics and figured he is mentally ready for school but not emotionally. My husband and I try to encourage learning and we had discouraged reading but now I'll get him books from the library if he wants them and will forget what people say, and they have said plenty. Incidentally, the two older children say they didn't help him.
>
> Thank you very much and I will keep your article for all the critics, especially sisters-in-law who also happen to be school teachers.

[15] This is a reference to a newspaper description of findings from this first study. It was the newspaper article that prompted this mother to write the letter.

Another impression left by the research interviews in California had to do with the easy availability of instructional materials for preschool children. While some of the materials described in the interviews were as "school-like" as the basal readers, many more were the picture dictionaries, the alphabet books, and even the workbooks that can be purchased in almost any food, toy, or department store. The abundance of these inexpensive materials found in the homes of the early readers certainly provoked curiosity about what would be found in the homes of children who did not learn to read before starting first grade.

Related to this new awareness of easily acquired instructional materials was increased awareness of the "word and number world" in which young children live. Quite frankly, it was only after doing the interviewing for the first study that this writer felt consciously attuned to the heavy dosage of numbers appearing on street signs, elevators, television dials, receipts, clocks, license plates, advertisements, calendars, and so on. Too, it was only after the interviews that the writer experienced a conscious and keen awareness of the abundance of words surrounding a child—on the television screen; on packaged and canned goods; on billboards and highway signs, storefronts and service stations; on cars and trucks; on toys, phonograph records, newspapers, and magazines. The question, then, that kept repeating itself was: Why don't more children learn to read before the first grade? For this researcher, it was one of the questions that suggested the need for the second study of early reading, a study in which the preschool years of both early readers and non-early-readers would be examined.

Pertinent to this second study were still other facts identified in the first one. Among these was the great interest in learning to print shown by the early readers in California. Actually, according to their parents' recollections of how they started reading, 10 of the 49 children first learned to print, then to spell, and only then to read. Of relevance here is the additional fact that all but one of the early readers entered first grade already able to print. The one child who could not do so had been eager to learn before the first grade, but was not allowed to try because her mother did not know "the right way to do it."

In general, then, the children identified as early readers in California were children who could also be described as early "scribblers." They were children who appeared to have advanced from aimless scribbling to the drawing of people and objects, and then to the making of letters copied most often from alphabet books, school papers of older siblings, and small blackboards. It is probably not an accident that in every one of the 49 families interviewed, a blackboard was available—often because it had belonged to an older child in the family, or because it had been purchased as effortlessly and cheaply as "up at the drug store for ninety-eight cents."

One other impression that probably ought to be reported here was what seemed like a minimal influence of the kindergarten on the interests of the children in this first study. For example, not one of the 47 parents who had sent their children to kindergarten expressed the belief that the kindergarten year had influenced or added to their children's interest in matters like reading or spelling or writing. While all of the parents showed appreciation for the genuine concern of the children's kindergarten teachers, almost half (23) also wondered why the kindergarten program had not extended the abilities their children already had in reading and spelling and writing.

This apparent cleavage between what the children could and did do at home, and what they were encouraged and allowed to do in kindergarten, raised many questions about the function of the kindergarten year in the lives of today's children. But more will be said about these matters in a later chapter.

Chapter V

California Case Studies

Even when case studies are brief and sketchy—as they are in this chapter
—they still assemble data in such a way that persons, rather than "subjects," emerge from the compilation. It was in the hope of conveying
some of this human quality that the present chapter was prepared.

The early readers selected for case studies are the children who had
the lowest and the highest Stanford–Binet IQ's at the beginning of grade
one; and the children who had the lowest and the highest reading achievement scores, also at the beginning of grade one. Actually, four subjects
met the criterion of having the lowest achievement; each began first grade
with a reading grade-level score of 1.5. Two of the four were randomly
selected for inclusion in the case studies.

The presentation of each case study begins with information about
the subject's race and sex, socioeconomic status, chronological age and
intelligence quotient at the beginning of grade one, and reading grade-
level scores at the beginning and end of the research. Fictitious names
are used.

Lowest IQ: ARLENE   Negro girl: UL socioeconomic status;
$CA = 6.9$; $IQ = 91$; initial reading grade $= 2.9$;
terminal reading grade $= 6.9$.

Arlene was the youngest of the three children in her family. At
the time of the research interview—Arlene was then in first grade—the
two older brothers were twelve and fourteen years of age. In describing
the family, Arlene's mother mentioned many times that she had always
wanted a daughter and that, from the time Arlene was born, she became
"her whole life."

59

Probably the different backgrounds of Arlene's parents also helped to create the close mother–daughter relationship to which frequent reference was made in the interview. Arlene's mother, according to her own report, was from "a family of teachers." She was quick to mention, too, that she herself had always been both a good student and an avid reader, and that she had just been completing the second year of college at the time of her marriage. With her marriage, she left school—something, she said, she had always regretted.

According to his wife's report, Arlene's father had been a poor student, and was able to complete only eight years of formal education. At the time of the research interview he was employed in a tire factory. Arlene's mother said he had "no interest in intellectual things," and that he spent much of his free time "playing in a little band."

It became quite obvious from answers to interview questions that much of the mother's free time was spent with Arlene. For example, the mother said she read to her daughter with great frequency, and in such a way that Arlene could see the pages. The mother felt this was one reason why Arlene, as early as age two, asked so many questions about the words being read.

The mother also mentioned that there was a large number of children's books available in her home, and that these included a variety of alphabet books and picture dictionaries. It was these two latter books that were used when mother and daughter played school together. Asked about the age at which Arlene first played school at home, the mother said, "It seems she's been playing school all her life." The mother felt that such an interest was "only natural" because, from the time Arlene could remember, her brothers were both attending school.

Another factor interpreted by the mother as one that fostered a "school at home" was the great disappointment felt by both Arlene and herself when the public school refused to accept Arlene for kindergarten, even though she missed the entrance cut-off date by only eight days. As a kind of consolation, the mother explained, she and Arlene played school at home for some part of most mornings. In this way, the mother said, she taught Arlene the names of letters and colors. She also identified words in the various alphabet books, and sometimes talked with Arlene about the sounds of letters. For this, the mother explained, she followed the pages in a phonics workbook which she purchased after seeing it advertised in a PTA magazine. She said they never did any printing—even though Arlene asked to learn—because she herself did not know "the right way to do it."

When asked whether she thought parents should teach preschool children such skills as reading, Arlene's mother was quick to respond affirmatively. She said that both of her sons had encountered difficulty in learning to read in school, probably because "teachers have so many in school, they don't have enough time for each child." The mother said she regretted following the advice of teachers who had told her that helping the boys with their reading at home would only lead to confusion. Now, she said, she was convinced this was not likely, and so she never hesitated to respond to Arlene's preschool curiosity about written words.

Arlene's mother also mentioned that she was much pleased with her daughter's early accomplishments because she did not want any of her children to be "dumb." She emphasized that the preschool learning certainly had not dimmed her daughter's interest in first grade, since Arlene was always eager to go to school, even when ill. The mother added, though, that the only new learning for Arlene at this point in first grade (December) was her ability to print.

Highest IQ: CAROL   Caucasian girl; UM socioeconomic status;
                       CA = 6.6; IQ = 161; initial reading grade = 2.8;
                                     terminal reading grade = 11.8.

At the start of the research interview, Carol's mother said she was aware of her daughter's ability to read "some words" before the first grade, but she was unable to describe exactly how Carol had learned them. The mother pointed out that neither she nor her husband, both college graduates, had ever tried to teach Carol to read because they believed "the school should do that kind of teaching." By the time the interview ended, however, Carol's mother was commenting about the way the interview questions clarified how Carol had begun to read early. In addition, she said, the questions also helped to explain why her older son had not been a preschool reader.

Answers to interview questions indicated that Carol had been read to, by both mother and father, "since about the age of two." Carol's only sibling, a brother, had been four at that time. The mother commented that both children "loved to be read to," and that when she herself did the reading she always tried to hold the book in such a way that the children could see the pictures. Carol, unlike her brother, was also interested in the words, and often asked her mother, "Where are you reading?" or "What word says that?"

The mother also recalled Carol's very special interest in *The Cat in the Hat*,[1] a book both parents read to the children so often that "Carol practically memorized the whole thing." The mother believed this book in particular had done much to encourage her daughter's already great interest in the sounds of words. The mother mentioned that Carol could often be heard around the house "playing with sounds, and making up things that weren't even words."

Interview responses indicated it was not only while being read to by their parents that Carol and her brother spent time together. The mother said there were no children living on their block who were Carol's age, and so Carol often played with her brother and his friends. On days

1 Geisel, Theodor Seuss. *The Cat in the Hat*, New York: Random House, 1957.

when the weather was inclement, the two children generally spent their time in a playroom. And, after the brother started first grade, the mother recalled, the playroom became a kind of classroom in which the six-year-old brother was the teacher and his four-year-old sister was the student.

A visit to this playroom showed not only toys, a television set, and an old piano, but also a great variety of materials which had obvious instructional potential. There were about 75 books, some of which were alphabet books and picture dictionaries. There were school-like workbooks, a blackboard, and an abundance of pencils and paper. There were coloring books that had captions beneath the pictures and, sometimes, simple directions for how the pictures were to be colored. There were games that required the matching of pictures and words, and there were stencils for tracing the letters of the alphabet.

In the interview, the mother mentioned that Carol made many more comments about this "school at home" than she ever made about either kindergarten or first grade. She said her daughter rarely talked about school, that in fact she seemed "quite unconcerned." However, the mother also said that Carol continued to be very much interested in reading, and was often found reading in bed at times when her parents had thought she was asleep for the night.

Toward the end of first grade, this writer spoke with Carol herself. When asked who it was who had first taught her to read, she answered, "I think I did it by sounding out words myself." She also said that she liked school very much ("except when the teacher blows up"), and that she was then reading in a second-grade book. Carol also mentioned that she read "three or four times a day" at home, and that she often went to the library for more books. She said, too, that her mother read as much as she did.

Lowest Initial
Reading Achievement: PAUL   Negro boy; UL socioeconomic status;
                                           CA = 6.4; IQ = 109; initial reading grade = 1.5;
                                                  terminal reading grade = 7.9.

Paul was among the four subjects who started first grade with a reading-grade score of 1.5. Toward the end of grade one, this writer asked Paul who it was who had initially taught him to read; and he responded, "My first-grade teacher."

In the family interview, held in November of the year Paul was in grade one, his mother explained that it was a combination of people who had helped Paul to read early, chiefly by answering his many persistent questions about words that interested him. In time, the mother said, she herself grew tired of "running to Paul to see what word he was asking about," and so she encouraged him to spell out the word, and she would tell him what it was. According to his mother, Paul knew the names of most of the letters by the time he was four. In this instance, the letters on his alphabet blocks, and the letters "at the top of an old blackboard belonging to his brother," were the initial sources of a curiosity about letter names.

Even before he was four, however, Paul was being read to by both parents. Paul's father, a school janitor, read to him "about two or three times a week." Paul's mother read stories "just about daily." Both parents read in such a way that Paul "could see the pictures."

Paul's mother said that neither she nor her husband ever deliberately planned to teach their son to read early because they felt "no special need for it." The mother said she had "no complaints" about the way the school taught reading, although she also mentioned that she had to help the older of her two children with his school work. This other son was four years older than Paul.

According to the mother, Paul first showed interest in participating in his brother's "homework sessions" at about the age of four. At that time, the brother was eight. The mother said Paul would "color, print, and ask questions" while she helped the older son. This was just one of the many ways, the mother pointed out, in which Paul tried very hard to "keep up" with his brother. She believed this persistent eagerness to match the accomplishments of his brother was the key factor in stimulating Paul's preschool interest in both reading and writing. However, she also expressed the belief that Paul's shyness would "get in the way of his learning in school." She said his attendance at kindergarten "helped a little," and that he had "adjusted nicely." She mentioned, too, that she was very pleased that Paul appeared to be happy with first grade, and that he seemed "especially interested in reading."

**Lowest Initial
Reading Achievement:** [2] SUSAN   Oriental girl; LM socioeconomic status;
CA = 6.7; IQ = 125; initial reading grade = 1.5;
terminal reading grade = 10.1.

The reason, of course, for interviewing Susan's parents was to collect information about the way she learned to read prior to first grade. What became obvious as the interview progressed, however, was that both parents were more eager to talk about the accomplishments of Susan's older brother, John.

At the time of the interview (October), Susan's father was just beginning a year of postgraduate studies at a divinity school. He was a Protestant minister, and had taken the year off for further study. Although Susan's mother was present for all of the interview, it was the father who responded to most of the interview questions. And in most of his responses, the son John was mentioned. It was fortunate that the

---

[2] As was noted in the opening of this chapter, 4 early readers had an initial grade-level score of 1.5. Two of these—Paul and Susan—were randomly selected for the case studies.

comments about this "very precocious child" also supplied information about the way Susan learned to read early.

Susan was one of three children. John was two years older, and a second brother was two years younger. The parents were natives of China, and both English and Chinese were spoken in the home.

That this home was one which valued academic accomplishments was immediately obvious. The mother was especially interested in the musical education of her children, although she said she "learned early that children can't be forced to like music." The father seemed well acquainted with the school his two oldest children attended; and, in all of his comments, admiration was shown for the competence of their teachers. The father mentioned, in the course of the interview, that his older son could easily have been reading before the first grade, but that his kindergarten teacher had said it was not wise for parents to try to teach their children to read. This teacher had emphasized, instead, the value of providing young children with a variety of experiences. It was for this reason, the father explained, that he took the children—as often as he had free time—to museums, the park, and the library. According to the father, it was also the kindergarten teacher's advice which made him "stay away from formal instruction" at home.

In speaking of his son, the father said, "Even though John only knew the alphabet when he started first grade, he learned to read without any trouble." More important for this research is the fact that John's quick achievement in first grade also provided the impetus and the opportunity for his four-year-old sister to learn to read early.

In the interview, both parents mentioned that Susan and John had shown interest in letters and words at an early age, but that Susan's interest had become especially obvious and persistent when her brother started to learn to read in first grade. At that time she was four years old.

The first thing Susan wanted to learn, the father said, was how to print. In the beginning, she would copy words from the papers John brought home from school, and then she would ask, "What do these say?" The father said his daughter had always been a "scribbler," and that even before she was four she had enjoyed drawing pictures and making up stories about them. "Her imagination was amazing," the father commented at one point in the interview.

As John became more advanced in his reading, Susan's father recalled, he also became more eager to "show his sister how to read." Both parents said the two older children often played school together, and that Susan did not seem to mind the chastisement of John when she made mistakes. "Susan always had respect for her brother," the father remarked.

It was while John was in first grade that another kind of "tutoring" also took place in this family. During that year an aunt and her three children arrived from China, and occupied an apartment in the building in which Susan and John lived. When the three cousins started school, Susan's father explained, they had great difficulty adjusting to the new language. Consequently, to help them learn to speak and read English, the school gave each child a large picture dictionary. Here, again, the father said, "John came to the rescue." Using the picture dictionaries and some of his own books, he conducted "a kind of school" for his older cousins; and Susan was "allowed to watch." The father said he was unable to identify what Susan learned from watching and asking questions, but that "probably she picked up a few things." The father was quick to mention that he himself continued to answer any questions about words or about spelling that Susan might ask. But he said he also avoided what he called "formal instruction." Here, again, he mentioned that he always kept in mind what John's kindergarten teacher had said about the inadvisability of parents teaching their children to read, and that he did not want to be the cause of any "school problems" for Susan.

Highest Initial
Reading Achievement: DONNA   Caucasian girl; UL socioeconomic status;
CA $= 6.7$; IQ $= 151$; initial reading grade $= 4.6$;
terminal reading grade $= 10.7$.

Donna was one of the 15 subjects in this research who were double-promoted. She also was one of the 11 subjects who were given help at home by someone who deliberately tried to teach reading (see Table 6). In the case of Donna, the "teacher" was her mother.

Donna's mother appeared to be a very quiet, easy-going person. She seemed to accept Donna's advanced and early achievement in reading in a matter-of-fact way and even commented, "The children in her class will soon catch up with her."

When asked how Donna learned to read early, the mother said that she herself "gave her a start." Answers to other interview questions emphasized that Donna, as a preschooler, "had to learn to play alone" because there were no children her age living in the neighborhood. As a result, the mother explained, Donna was always seeking out "things that could be done by one person." The mother mentioned, in the interview, that Donna sometimes played with her younger brother—"whenever he was willing to be bossed"—but, generally, "he got in her hair."

Before Donna was old enough for kindergarten, the mother recalled, she began to insist that "someone show her how to read." The mother said she probably picked up this interest "from watching her older brother and sister devour comic books." Even earlier, though, Donna had learned the names of the letters of the alphabet from listening to an alphabet song on a phonograph record. She also had learned to print most of the letters by copying them "many times" from a "teach yourself" printing book which had been used earlier by a brother and a sister. At the time of the interview, these siblings were twelve and thirteen, respectively.

Donna's mother said that once she herself had decided to try to teach Donna to read, she then wondered "how to go about it." When she went to a department store to see what materials might be available, the clerk suggested a phonics workbook for children. The clerk said it was a book "the school approved of."

"From the first page to the last, Donna enjoyed what we did," the mother recalled. She also explained that they "followed one page after another," but only worked "when Donna wanted to." And "In no time at all, she was reading on her own." After that, the mother said, they went to the library "about every other week," and the librarian selected books which Donna could read. Here the mother recalled how Donna would often take books with her when she went outdoors to play.

During the interview, Donna's mother expressed no surprise at the ease with which her younger daughter had learned to read. At one point she said, "That's the way she is with everything." And then the mother cited, as an example, the way Donna had quickly learned "some very long prayers when she was only two or three." Later in the interview the mother remarked, "Donna and my oldest daughter have a memory just like their father's."

At other times, when the mother characterized Donna, she described her as "a nice little girl"; as a child who "wants to go beyond herself and is always accepting challenges to do more and to do better"; as one who is "not a cocky kid but very sure of herself"; and as "her father's pet."

Donna's father, an appliance repairman, "took great delight," the mother said, "in reading to Donna." For as long as the mother could remember, "He read to her every single night," and this was always "a special time for both of them." Even after Donna had begun to read herself, the father still read to her every night before she went to bed. Now Donna seemed especially pleased "to hear him read what she had already read."

Toward the end of this interview Donna's mother was asked: "Do you think a child should be taught to read only by a trained person?" In response, she said, "I certainly thought so at one time, but now I don't think so because Donna has done so well." Several times during the interview the mother said it never would have occurred to her to teach any of her children to read, but that Donna had "begged" her. Donna was "always looking for things to do." The mother mentioned, too, that she had "no regrets" about helping Donna, but she also expressed the belief that parents who decide to help their children to read at home "should go according to some book or plan."

Chapter **VI**

The Second Study:
New York City

Reasons for this second study of early readers have been mentioned intermittently in reporting the first study. Now they will be brought together and made more explicit.

The primary and most compelling reason for the second study was the lack of data, in the first one, about children who do not read early. Lacking comparative data, the initial study only could arrive at tentative conclusions about factors that seem especially significant in fostering preschool reading. Consequently, the second study was designed to investigate the preschool years of both early readers and non-early-readers. This second phase of the research also attempted to ascertain whether certain personality characteristics would be apparent in both groups.

Another major reason for the second longitudinal study was the hope that better testing procedures would yield more valid data for reading achievement and for intelligence. In the first study, it will be recalled, achievement comparisons of early readers and non-early-readers depended upon school-administered tests. As a result, intelligence data for two of the comparisons were obtained from a group test, and for the other comparison from an individual test which had been administered to the control group by the schools. Because school systems often need to reserve the use of individual intelligence tests for children who are somewhat deviant either in behavior or achievement or both, it is possible that the control group in this particular comparison might not have been representative of a typical school population.

Data for the reading achievement comparisons in the first study were not the most valid either. Especially for the advanced readers in both the experimental and the control groups, doubts were raised about the adequacy of the reading tests used by the schools.

67

Testing Plans for the Second Study

Because of these testing problems, plans for the second study included use of the *Stanford–Binet Intelligence Scale* with both early readers and non-early-readers. Now, and for both groups of children, the data would come not from school records but from testing which was a part of the total research plan.

Plans for the second study also included the use, with both groups, of a series of reading tests which would be easy enough for the less advanced readers but sufficiently difficult to identify upper limits of achievement for the best readers.

Essentially, then, changes planned for the second study were related more to research procedures than to research questions. In this second study, concern was still for the following questions:

What is the effect of early reading on subsequent achievement in reading?

What kinds of factors, either within a family or about a child himself, foster preschool reading?

Do any of these factors have implications for beginning school instruction in reading?

Before a description is given of the way subjects for the second phase of the research were identified and studied, attention should be directed to what was happening to the educational world between the starting date of the first study (September, 1958) and the time the second study began (September, 1961). A quick survey of some developments —in particular, of the development of thought regarding readiness for learning—will outline the educational setting in which the second study was started. In certain important ways, this setting was different from that of the first study.

Some Developments between 1958 and 1961

In 1958, it will be recalled, there was general acceptance of the value of, and even the need for, reading readiness programs in the beginning weeks or months of the first-grade year. There appeared, too, to be fairly general acceptance of a mental age of 6.5 as a prerequisite for beginning reading. Also apparent was a reliance on reading readiness tests to predict a child's success. And finally, it is accurate to say, 1958 was part of an era in which the schools generally discouraged early home help with reading, and in which parents were warned that preschool help would lead to problems of confusion, or of boredom, when school instruction began.

In September, 1961, the second longitudinal study of early reading was started. What kind of educational practice and thought predominated at that time? While it is extremely difficult to know exactly what goes on in classrooms, it is the opinion of this writer that practice in early childhood education in 1961 reflected the educational thought of 1958. However, between 1958 and 1961 there was some stirring and some change in psychological beliefs about young children in general, and about their readiness for learning in particular.

One of the most highly publicized books about young children and readiness appeared in 1960. Called *The Process of Education,* and written by the psychologist Jerome Bruner, this book discussed the general topic of readiness in one of its chapters [13]. The chapter included a pronouncement that was quoted later with great frequency: ". . . any subject can be taught effectively in some intellectually honest form to any child at any stage of development." Within the framework of the total book, this pronouncement had a meaning that was not too startling. When quoted out of context, however, the proposal was susceptible to much misinterpretation. At times, it was quoted to raise questions that needed to be asked. At other times, it seems fair to say, the pronouncement fostered what could only be called propaganda about the learning potential of young children.

Earlier, in a 1959 article in the *Teachers College Record,* another psychologist had discussed readiness, taking issue with the school's interpretation of the readiness concept [5]. The general thesis of this article by David P. Ausubel was that "premature and wholesale extension of developmental principles to educational theory and practice has caused incalculable harm." The author expressed the opinion that "It will take at least a generation for teachers to unlearn some of the more fallacious and dangerous of these overgeneralized and unwarranted applications."

One such application, according to Ausubel, was the school's use of the readiness concept. Ausubel acknowledged that an interpretation of readiness which supports the idea that attained capacity affects what is gained by current experience or practice is "empirically demonstrable and conceptually unambiguous." He was concerned to show, however, that difficulty arises when readiness is equated with maturation:

> To equate the principles of readiness and maturation not only muddies the conceptual waters but also makes it difficult for the school to appreciate that insufficient readiness may reflect inadequate prior learning on the part of pupils because of inappropriate or inefficient instructional methods. Lack of maturation can thus become a convenient scapegoat whenever children manifest insufficient readiness to learn, and the school, which is thereby automatically absolved of all responsibility in the matter, consequently fails to subject its instructional practices to the degree of self-critical scrutiny necessary for continued educational progress. In short, while it is important to appreciate that the current readiness of pupils determines the school's current choice of instructional methods and materials, it is equally important

to bear in mind that this readiness itself is partly determined by the appropriateness and efficiency of the previous instructional practices to which they have been subjected. [5:248]

Discussing the readiness concept in relation to age, Ausubel referred to the effect of Gesell's work on the popular view:

> It is hardly surprising, in view of the tremendous influence on professional and lay opinion wielded by Gesell and his colleagues, that many people conceive of readiness in absolute and immutable terms, and thus fail to appreciate that except for such traits as walking and grasping, the mean ages of readiness can never be specified apart from relevant environmental conditions. [5:249]

Later, Ausubel discussed the relationship of age to reading readiness in particular. The following sentence is of special interest because of the findings from the first study reported in this monograph:

> Middle-class children, for example, are ready to read at an earlier age than lower-class children because of the greater availability of books in the home and because they are read to and taken places more frequently. [5:249]

Another psychologist, this time in 1961, raised still further questions about traditional notions regarding such factors as experience, readiness, and intelligence. J. McV. Hunt, in his widely circulated book *Intelligence and Experience*, offered new interpretations of some of the early studies involved in the classical nature–nurture controversy [48]. Of special relevance to educators of young children was Hunt's claim that "the rate of development is in substantial part, but certainly not wholly, a function of environmental circumstances . . . . Thus, the greater the variety of situations to which the child must accommodate his behavioral structures, the more differentiated and mobile they become." In a sense, Hunt was saying what Ausubel emphasized in the article mentioned earlier.

While psychologists like Ausubel, Hunt, and Bruner were raising questions about conventional explanations of human growth and development, voices from other sources also were being heard between 1958 and 1961. For instance, in a 1960 issue of *Harper's Magazine*, a private school teacher asked, "Why Waste Our Five-Year-Olds?" [88]. This teacher maintained that early education in this country was "a holding-back procedure," that kindergartens were duplicating nursery schools, and that five-year-olds were "capable of more than play."

In another popular magazine, a 1960 article highlighted the successful efforts of a sociologist to teach preschool children to type, read, and write, with the assistance of computerized typewriters. The magazine was *Time* [28], and the sociologist was O. K. Moore.

During this same period, other popular magazine articles excited the public about the revival of Montessori education in the United States [16, 74]. Of particular interest was the Whitby School in Connecticut. The popular press especially emphasized Whitby's demonstration of the learnings of three- and four-year-old children when Montessori method and curriculum were followed.

But what about public school educators during this period? It can be said that they were neither silent nor in perfect unison. And neither silence nor agreement would have been natural during these years, for they were part of the post-Sputnik era.

The launching of Sputnik I, on October 4, 1957, produced a variety of repercussions in the United States. One was criticism that pounced on public school education, increasing the tempo of the already existing debate about the quality of instruction in American schools [9]. The debate now stressed the inferiority of our educational endeavors compared to those of Soviet Russia [7, 27]. Resulting from the clamor was an atmosphere best characterized by the cry of "Let's have more and let's have it sooner." These demands, coupled with new messages from psychologists, were bound to have an effect on early childhood education.

In 1960, for instance, the Educational Policies Commission of the National Education Association was writing:

> The kindergarten is designed for five-year-olds. Its central purpose is to help the young child adapt to school, to find his place in school life and in the group of which he is a member, and to promote readiness for learning in various areas. It helps him gain independence and social maturity. It works through activities appropriate to a school setting, but adapted to the immaturity and restlessness of the young child. [29:11]

However, the same Commission, and in the same report, was also saying:

> The kindergarten can and should teach reading when such teaching contributes to the goals of the kindergarten. And development of desire and readiness to read in all children is a proper function of the kindergarten, for this contributes to its central purpose. [29:11]

More typical of professionals who specialized in early childhood education was a posture of "defense" of the young child. This reaction is apparent in a 1960 article by two professors of education:

> Recently pressure has been exerted to redesign the kindergarten program to attain fixed academic standards. The anxieties and tensions of our times create a sense of urgency that is likely to be transferred to the kindergarten child if we do not exercise caution. [62:59]

A similar attitude is even more openly expressed in another 1960 article—in *Childhood Education,* a publication of the Association for Childhood Education International:

The restlessness and anxiety of our times have been expressed in trying to force down in the curriculum learnings for which the child is neither physiologically or psychologically ready and for which he sees no need. We have a mountain of evidence to prove that a perfectly "normal" child—I.Q. 100—cannot learn to read until he is about six years six months old. Any attempt to drive him may result in some evidence of reading but at an excessive cost in physiological and psychological damage and at great risk of impairment of his interest in reading. When the time comes he can master it readily. [44:316]

These brief references to certain developments between 1958 and 1961, as reflected in educational journals, psychology texts, and popular magazines, are enough to give at least a sketchy picture of the setting in which this writer's second study of early readers began. Remaining sections in the chapter will describe how subjects for the new research were identified and then studied for a period of three years.

Location of the Second Study

During the time of preparation for the second study, this researcher was on the faculty of Teachers College, Columbia University. The move away from the University of California required a corresponding change in the location of the new study.

Initially, the intent was to locate the research in a city similar to Oakland in size and in heterogeneous population. Three communities close to New York City had the heterogeneity, although the populations were smaller. Meetings were arranged with the school superintendents in these cities to discuss the possibility of carrying on the study in their schools. As it happened, all three of the superintendents refused permission, and for the same reason. The kind of research proposed, they said, would "stir up trouble" in the community. One of the superintendents put it this way: "I have enough problems already. No thanks."

Fortunately, these negative and discouraging reactions also had their blessings. For one thing, they made this writer even more grateful for the very professional cooperation of the Oakland schools. Later, and by contrast, they highlighted the enthusiastic approval of the research given by the New York City public school system.[1] For the second study, then, the location was to be New York City.

Selection of Schools

In New York, the expected first-grade enrollment for September, 1961, was 75,000 children. Because of the immense size of the group, the original plan to identify subjects from a total first-grade population was abandoned. Instead, and with the very careful assistance of the New

[1] Here, the writer gratefully acknowledges the support and cooperation of Dr. John B. King, Mrs. Helene M. Lloyd, and Dr. J. Wayne Wrightstone.

York City Bureau of Research, 40 schools were selected. The schools were located in Manhattan, Queens, Brooklyn, and the Bronx.

In choosing schools, one of the goals was to have a population of about 5,000 first-grade children. Such a population would be comparable in size to the Oakland group from which subjects for the first study had been identified.

The second goal in selecting New York schools was to have a total group of schools which represented an equal distribution among the different socioeconomic classes. In New York City, of course, this meant including in the testing many Puerto Rican children whose native language would be Spanish. But this difficulty had to be accepted: the heterogeneity with regard to socioeconomic status was important because of the concern in the second study for the kinds of factors that are associated with early reading. While there is no pretense to perfect achievement of this goal of heterogeneity, it can be maintained that the 40 selected schools in New York City varied greatly in the socioeconomic backgrounds of their students.

Population to Be Tested

As in the original study, certain first-grade children in the 40 New York schools were excluded from the testing which was used to identify subjects. Children spending their second year in the first grade were not tested, nor were the children described as getting even a small amount of help with reading during the kindergarten year. With these two groups of first-graders eliminated, the remaining first-grade population in the 40 schools numbered 4,465 children—2,324 boys and 2,141 girls. Racially, the total group was comprised of 3,523 Caucasians, 814 Negroes, and 128 Orientals.

Identification of Early Readers

Subjects for the second study were identified by means of the same two-step testing procedure that was used in the California study. In the beginning, the 37-word test (see Appendix A) was administered, individually and orally, to the 4,465 children. Of this group, 180 children, or about 4 per cent of the total group tested, were successful in identifying a minimum of 18 words. These 180 children attended 35 schools.

Next, each of the 180 potential subjects was given the Gates *Primary Word Recognition* and *Primary Paragraph Reading* tests (Form 1, 1958 Edition). Results showed that 23 of the potential subjects were unable to achieve a raw score of at least 1 on the more difficult of the two tests, the *Primary Paragraph Reading.* Consequently they were eliminated as subjects because, as in the first study, an early reader was considered to be a child who read well enough at the beginning of grade one to score on both of these standardized tests.

Of the 157 first graders who were able to score on both the *Primary*

Word Recognition and *Primary Paragraph Reading* tests, 10 children missed only 2 or fewer items in the more difficult of the two tests. Following the procedures of the first study, these 10 children were then given the Gates *Advanced Primary Word Recognition* and *Advanced Primary Paragraph Reading* tests (Form 1, 1958 Edition).

With the help of very cooperative principals, teachers, research assistants, and a wide variety of subway trains and buses, all of this testing was completed within the first two weeks of the first grade, prior to the start of school instruction in reading.

Brief Description of the Early Readers

Even before the third week of the semester began, the family of one of the 157 New York early readers moved to another state. Because this second phase of the research no longer was concerned with the frequency of reading achievement among beginning first graders, this early reader was eliminated from the research. As a result, the early readers for the second study numbered 156 children who were enrolled in 33 schools located in four boroughs. Other information about the 156 subjects, as they compared with the population from which they were identified, is summarized in Table 15.

Table 15. The 156 early readers compared with the first-grade populations from which they were selected

| Population Tested | | Early Readers | |
NUMBER	DESCRIPTION	NUMBER	PER CENT OF POPULATION TESTED
4,465	Total group	156	3.5
2,324	Boys	76	3.3
2,141	Girls	80	3.7
3,523	Caucasians	139	3.9
814	Negroes	12	1.5
128	Orientals	5	3.9

Results of the standardized reading tests which were used in identifying the 156 subjects showed median scores ranging from 1.4 to 5.2, according to grade-level norms. The median grade-level score for the group was 2.0. Results of the *Stanford–Binet Intelligence Scale* (Form L-M, 1960 Edition), administered soon after subjects were identified, showed intelligence quotients that varied from 82 to 170. The median intelligence quotient was 133.[2]

[2] Stanford–Binet IQ scores achieved by the subjects in this first year are used throughout the report to describe their intelligence.

This brief description of the 156 early readers also must include the fact that the children turned out to be "travelers." At the start of the study, the early readers were enrolled in 33 New York City public schools. By the end of the first year, however, 5 of the 156 had transferred to public schools in other cities, while one child was attending a New York City private school.

At the end of the second year of the research, 14 early readers were attending public schools in other cities, while 4 were enrolled in 4 different New York City private schools. This left 138 children in New York public schools, but not all of the 138 still were attending the schools in which they had been identified as early readers.

By the time the study was concluded after three years, it had become international. One early reader was attending school in Toronto, Canada; another was in Tokyo, Japan. Of the 154 early readers who remained in the United States, only 125 still attended New York City public schools; 7 children were enrolled in New York City private schools, 20 were enrolled in public school systems in other cities, and 2 were attending parochial schools.

Testing Procedures for the
156 Early Readers

To follow the reading progress of the 156 subjects over a three-year period, testing procedures in this second study paralleled those used in the California research. There was one change, however, as will be seen.

The *Gates Reading Tests* (1958 Edition) include four series of tests: (1) *Primary Reading Tests,* (2) *Advanced Primary Reading Tests,* (3) *Basic Reading Tests,* and (4) *Reading Survey.* The subtests included in the testing plan for the New York study were the following:

Test	Reading-Grade Range
PRIMARY	
Primary Word Recognition (PWR)	1.4— 3.7
Primary Paragraph Reading (PPR)	1.4— 4.4
ADVANCED PRIMARY	
Advanced Primary Word Recognition (AWR)	1.8— 5.8
Advanced Primary Paragraph Reading (APR)	1.8— 6.2
BASIC	
Reading Vocabulary (RV)	2.0—12.6
Level of Comprehension (LC)	2.0—12.5
SURVEY	
Reading Vocabulary	2.1—12.8
Level of Comprehension	2.1—12.5

In the test manuals, it is noted that the *Reading Survey* "may be used as a somewhat more economical substitute" for the *Basic Reading*

Tests [32]. For the California study it was this suggestion that prompted the use of two of the *Survey* subtests, following the *Advanced Primary* tests. However, it will be recalled that the grade-level scores of the California subjects consistently declined as they moved from the level of the *Advanced Primary* tests to that of the *Survey* (see page 22). It was postulated, therefore, that the *Basic* series might be more suitable than the *Survey*, for these young children. (One reason for this was the larger type and more spacious format of the *Basic* Reading Vocabulary test; another was the writer's subjective impressions of the relative difficulty, for this age group, of the *Survey* vocabulary and subject matter.) Consequently, for the New York phase of the research it was decided to use two of the five *Basic* tests following the *Advanced Primary* tests.

Administration of reading tests, at one-year intervals, followed the guidelines used in the California study. In the beginning, each subject was given the PWR and PPR tests. From that point on, however, the tests for each subject at each testing period depended upon test performance. In all of the testing sessions, including the one in which subjects were identified, the following plan was adhered to by the research assistants who administered the tests.

Whenever a subject took the *Primary* (PWR and PPR) tests and missed 2 or fewer items in the more difficult (PPR), he then would be given the *Advanced Primary* (AWR and APR) tests. Whenever a subject took AWR and APR and missed 2 or fewer items in the more difficult of these two (APR), then the *Basic* RV and LC tests would be administered. If a subject taking RV and LC missed 2 or fewer items in LC, he would then be given the two subtests in the *Survey*. As it turned out, there was no need to use the *Survey* tests in the three-year New York study.

Again, in this New York study, the subjects' achievement in reading, at each testing period, was to be described by the median of all the grade-levels achieved in whatever tests they were qualified to take. The median was selected because it is a conservative estimate of reading achievement, as achievement was to be assessed in the research.

Selection of a Special Experimental Group

The major interest in the second study was to compare early readers and non-early-readers. A particular goal was the identification of possible similarities and differences in the preschool years of the two groups of children. Achievement of such a goal again required family interviews. Because of the impossibility of doing 312 extensive interviews (156 early readers and 156 non-early readers), it was decided to select 30 children from the group of 156 early readers. Following this, the selected group would be matched with a group of 30 non-early-readers. The families of the 60 children would then be interviewed by this researcher.

As a first step, therefore, 30 children were randomly selected from the group of 156 early readers. The selected group of 30, hereafter referred to as the special experimental group, was comprised of 19 boys and 11 girls who were attending 18 schools in four boroughs; 28 of the children were Caucasians, and 2 were Negroes.

On the basis of the standardized tests which had been used to identify subjects, the grade-level reading scores of this special experimental group ranged from 1.5 to 5.2, at the beginning of first grade. The median grade-level score was 2.1. (For the total group of 156 early readers, grade-level scores ranged from 1.4 to 5.2 The median score was 2.0.)

According to data derived from the *Stanford–Binet Intelligence Scale,* administered soon after subjects were identified, IQ's for these 30 early readers varied from 99 to 170. The median IQ was 132. (For the total group of 156 early readers, IQ scores ranged from 82 to 170, and the median IQ was 133.)

Selection of a Control Group

Because of the importance of mental ability to reading achievement, the first variable considered in selecting 30 non-early-readers was intelligence. Ideally, the matching of non-early-readers with the 30 early readers would be done on the basis of Stanford–Binet IQ's. However, because of the practical impossibility of this kind of matching, the decision instead was to use a two-step matching procedure. Initially, a control group would be selected on the basis of IQ scores derived from the *Pintner–Cunningham Intelligence Test* (Primary Test, Form A, 1938 Edition). This group intelligence test was administered by the New York City schools during the first semester of the first grade. Once 30 non-early-readers were selected on this basis, they would then be given the *Stanford–Binet Intelligence Scale.* If necessary, a rematching of the early readers and non-early-readers would be done on the basis of Stanford–Binet IQ's.

In selecting the 30 non-early-readers, hereafter referred to as the control group, the factors of sex and first-grade teacher also were considered. The total matching procedure, then, went as follows.

Teachers of the 30 children in the special experimental group were asked to select children in their classrooms who were of the same sex as the early readers and whose Pintner–Cunningham IQ's matched most closely the Pintner–Cunningham IQ's of the early readers. Once the 30 non-early-readers were selected, each was given the *Stanford–Binet Intelligence Scale* (Form L-M, 1960 Edition). Results of the testing showed IQ's ranging from 104 to 161. (IQ scores for the 30 early readers ranged from 99 to 170.) The median IQ for the control group was 132. (The median IQ for the 30 early readers was also 132.)

On the basis of Stanford–Binet IQ's, some of the early readers and non-early-readers were rematched in order to minimize IQ differences.

With this rematching, only 18 pairs of children continued to be paired on the basis of sex as well as IQ.

When the rematching was completed, the Stanford–Binet IQ's of each pair of children were compared, resulting in a difference score. Whenever the IQ of the early reader exceeded the IQ of the non-early-reader with whom he had been paired, the difference was noted as being positive. Whenever the non-early-reader's IQ was higher, the difference was recorded as a negative difference. Following this procedure, the 30 difference scores ranged from —5 to +9, with a mean difference of +2.6.[3] For 6 of the 30 pairs of children, IQ scores were identical.

Procedures for Studying the Control Group and the Special Experimental Group

To examine the effect of early reading on later achievement, reading tests were given each year to the 30 children in the control group, and to the 30 early readers in the special experimental group. Testing procedures duplicated those used with the total group of early readers (see page 76). Results of this testing will be reported in the next chapter, Chapter VII.

To identify possible differences and similarities in the preschool years of children in the control and experimental groups, home interviews were held with parents. Data from these 60 interviews will be reported in Chapter VIII.

To identify similarities and differences among the children themselves, a variety of procedures was followed during the three-year period of the research. With all 60 children, the following tests and scales were used: (1) a Teacher Rating Scale; (2) the Bender *Visual Motor Gestalt Test;* and (3) the *Minnesota Tests of Creative Thinking.* The rationale for using these various instruments, and the data they yielded, will be described in Chapter IX.

Chapter X presents some case studies of both early readers and non-early-readers, and Chapter XI describes very briefly some of the thinking about young children that prevailed in 1964, the year the second study was terminated. Chapter XII will conclude the report with a discussion of the findings from both studies.

[3] When the early readers and non-early-readers were initially matched on the basis of Pintner–Cunningham IQ's, the mean of the difference was +0.9.

Chapter VII

Reading Achievement
in the Second Study

The achievement of preschool readers, over time, was a concern of both studies described in this monograph. In the second study, however, major interest shifted more to identifying factors associated with early reading than to studying its effect on subsequent achievement. This was why the second study terminated after three years.

To be reported in this chapter are data from the second study that do deal with the effect of a head start in reading. In the beginning sections, the focus is on the reading progress of 156 early readers during a three-year period. Subsequent sections compare the progress of 30 of these early readers with the progress of 30 non-early-readers.

Test Results for 156 Early Readers

Table 16 summarizes the reading achievement of the 156 early readers in the New York study, over a three-year period, and also shows the relationship between achievement and intelligence, as intelligence was measured by the Stanford–Binet scale. Table 17 summarizes these intelligence data.

A comparison of the data which describe the reading progress of the 156 early readers in this second study (Table 16), and the data describing the progress of the 49 early readers in the California research (Table 1) shows some differences, even though similar testing procedures

Table 16. Reading progress of 156 early readers over a
three-year period, and the relationship between
progress and intelligence

Date of Testing	Reading Grade-Level		Correlation between Reading Achievement and Intelligence
	MEDIAN	RANGE	
Sept. 1961	2.0	1.4— 5.2	.24
May 1962	3.7	2.3— 7.2	.44
May 1963	5.1	3.0— 8.7	.52
May 1964	6.1	3.4—11.2	.44

Table 17. Stanford–Binet intelligence
data for the 156 early readers

Subjects	Intelligence Quotient	
	RANGE	MEDIAN
Boys and girls (N=156)	82—170	133
Boys (N=77)	82—163	133
Girls (N=79)	94—170	134

were used.[1] For example, in the first study the median grade-level score
for the 49 subjects at the beginning of grade one was 1.9; and three years
later it was 5.3. In this second study, the median grade-level score for
the 156 early readers was 2.0 at the start of first grade, and 6.1 three years
later.

One possible reason for the greater progress shown in the second
study is the higher intelligence of its subjects. The median Stanford–
Binet IQ for the 49 early readers in California was 121 (Table 2), and
for the 156 New York early readers it was 133 (Table 17). Here, though,
it should be reemphasized that the relationship between intelligence and
reading achievement was less pronounced in the New York study than
in the California research (see Tables 1 and 16). The correlation coefficient for achievement and intelligence at the end of three years was
.71 in California but only .44 in New York. However—and this fact will
be noted again (Table 19)—when the double-promoted early readers in
the New York study are considered as a separate group, then the correlation coefficient is .65.

[1] One difference between testing procedures, it will be recalled, was the use in
the New York study of Gates *Basic* tests following the Gates *Advanced Primary* tests.
It also turned out that the *Survey* was not needed in the three-year New York study.
Whether these differences helped to account for the less pronounced relationship between achievement and intelligence in the New York research is not known.

Test Results by Sex

Reading and intelligence data for the 156 early readers also were analyzed in relation to the sex of each subject. Results of the analysis are summarized in Table 18. An obvious trend in these data is the very close similarity in the reading progress of boys and of girls. Unlike the case in California, there is also similarity in the correlation coefficients for achievement and intelligence. In the California research, these were .58 for the boys and .78 for the girls, after three years. In this New York study, the coefficients were .44 for the boys and .48 for the girls.

Table 18. Reading progress of 77 male and 79 female early readers over a three-year period, and the relationship between progress and intelligence

| Date of Testing | Reading Grade-Level: | | | | Correlation between Reading Achievement and Intelligence | |
| | Range | | Median | | | |
	BOYS	GIRLS	BOYS	GIRLS	BOYS	GIRLS
Sept. 1961	1.4— 4.5	1.5— 5.2	2.1	2.0	.27	.22
May 1962	2.3— 5.4	2.5— 7.2	3.7	3.7	.50	.39
May 1963	3.0— 8.7	3.0— 7.6	5.0	5.1	.57	.47
May 1964	4.0—11.2	3.4—10.7	6.1	6.1	.44	.48

Comparison of Test Results for Double-Promoted and Non-Double-Promoted Early Readers

As in the first study, some early readers in this second one were double-promoted during the years of the research. More specifically, by the end of the third year, 25 of the 156 New York subjects had been accelerated, and so these children were in grade four when the study ended. There were 5 double promotions during the first year of the research; 9 other double promotions occurred during the second year; and the remaining 11 took place in the third year.

To facilitate comparisons of intelligence and reading achievement, data for both the double-promoted and the non-double-promoted early readers are presented in one table, Table 19. Comparisons show that again it was the brighter children who were double-promoted—although, in this New York study, median intelligence quotients for all of the various subgroups are high and closely similar. Further examination of Table 19 also indicates an advantage in achievement for the early readers who were accelerated. As in the California study (see Tables 4 and 5), the advantage is greater for the boys than for the girls.

As in the California study, too, the various correlation coefficients shown in Table 19 indicate more pronounced relationships between in-

Table 19. Reading achievement of non-double-promoted and double-promoted subjects after three years, and the relationship between achievement and intelligence

Subjects	Intelligence Quotient		Reading Grade-Level		Correlation: Reading Achievement and IQ
	MEDIAN	RANGE	MEDIAN	RANGE	
Total group					
Non-double-promoted (N=131)	133	82—162	5.8	3.4—11.2	.38
Double-promoted (N=25)	137	115—170	7.8	5.2—10.7	.65
Boys					
Non-double-promoted (N=63)	132	82—158	5.6	4.0—11.2	.39
Double-promoted (N=14)	135	118—163	8.7	5.2—10.4	.50
Girls					
Non-double-promoted (N=68)	133	94—162	6.0	3.4— 9.3	.38
Double-promoted (N=11)	137	115—170	7.0	5.3—10.7	.77

telligence and achievement for double-promoted early readers than for those who were not double-promoted. Unlike the case in California, however, this difference is greater for the girls than for the boys.

No matter how the achievement of the 156 early readers in this second study is analyzed, the findings are encouraging. Certainly none of the data in Tables 16, 18, and 19 indicate achievement problems for children who get a head start in reading.

Thus far, however, only data describing the progress of early readers have been presented. The next two sections of the chapter will report comparisons of the reading achievement of a selected group of 30 early readers with that of a group of 30 non-early-readers.

Achievement Comparisons of Early Readers and Non-Early-Readers

Each May, during the three-year period of the New York research, reading tests were administered to 30 early readers (special experimental group) and to the 30 non-early-readers paired with them on the basis of Stanford–Binet IQ's. To compare the reading achievement of these two groups of children, the following procedures were followed for each of the three years of the research.

First, the reading achievement of the early reader and the non-early-reader in each pair of children was compared; and the difference, in years, was determined. Whenever the difference favored an early reader, it was recorded as a positive difference; whenever it favored the non-early-reader, it was recorded as a negative difference. At the end of the first year of the research the 30 differences ranged in value from −1.1 to +4.2, with a mean difference of +1.0. At the end of the second year, the difference scores ranged from −0.8 to +3.5, with a mean difference of +1.0. At the conclusion of the research, the differences ranged in value from −2.9 to +5.6, with a mean difference of +0.9.

The statistical significance of the three mean difference scores was evaluated with one-tailed t tests of the null hypothesis. As in the first study, the null hypothesis would be rejected if the value of t was significant at the .05 level. Results of the tests are summarized in Table 20. They show that the average achievement of early readers was significantly higher than that of comparably bright non-early-readers, and that the lead was maintained over a three-year period.

Table 20. Reading achievement comparisons of a matched group of 30 early readers and 30 non-early-readers

Date of Testing	Mean Difference Scores in Years	Standard Deviation of Difference Scores	Value of t
May 1962	+1.0 [a]	1.2	4.6 [b]
May 1963	+1.0	1.3	4.2 [b]
May 1964	+0.9	2.4	2.1 [c]

[a] Positive difference scores indicate an advantage for the early readers.
[b] Significant at the .0005 level.
[c] Significant at the .025 level.

In making comparisons between the achievement of early readers and non-early-readers, one other factor merits explicit attention. It is the fact that among the 30 early readers in the special experimental group, 8 were double-promoted during the three-year period of the research. In contrast, none of the 30 children in the control group was accelerated. To examine the possible effect of double promotions on achievement, the following procedure was followed.

At the conclusion of the research, the mean of the difference scores involving the eight double-promoted early readers was calculated. It was found to be +2.3. This indicates that the average reading achievement of the eight double-promoted early readers exceeded by 2.3 years the average achievement of the non-early-readers with whom they were paired, after three years of school instruction in reading.

The mean of the 22 difference scores involving the non-double-promoted early readers also was calculated, and was found to be +0.8. This indicates that the average reading achievement of the 22 non-double-promoted early readers also exceeded the achievement of the 22 non-early-readers with whom they were paired, but only by .8 years.

In summary, then, two conclusions about these comparably bright groups of early readers and non-early-readers may be stated. First, the average reading achievement of the early readers was significantly higher than that of the non-early-readers, over a three-year period (see Table 20); and, secondly, the advantage in achievement seems especially pronounced for the early readers who were accelerated.

Achievement Comparisons when Early Readers and Non-Early-Readers Are Matched Statistically

The previous section has described the achievement of early readers and non-early-readers paired on the basis of Stanford–Binet IQ's. These children have been referred to as "comparably bright" groups even though the average IQ score of the early readers exceeded that of the non-early-readers by 2.6 points. Although this difference is small, it still prompts questions about its effect on data that have led to positive conclusions about the value of a head start in reading.

To respond to such questions, the correlations between the difference scores in achievement and the difference scores in intelligence were computed for each year. These correlations were relatively small, but positive (.39, .36, .31). The average difference in achievement scores for each year was adjusted by subtracting the predicted difference in achievement based on the differences in intelligence. The significance of these adjusted means was then evaluated by t tests.* The values of t for the 1962, 1963, and 1964 data were, respectively, 2.8, 2.4, and 2.1. All are significant at the .05 level. This leads to the conclusion that the average achievement of the 30 early readers is significantly higher than that of the 30 non-early-readers even when the two groups are statistically matched on IQ.

Advantage of Earlier Reading in Relation to Intelligence

The intelligence of the 30 early readers corresponded closely to that of the total group of 156 early readers from which they had been randomly selected. (Frequency distributions of IQ's for both groups are

$$* \, t(N-2) = \cfrac{\overline{Y} - b\overline{X}}{\sqrt{\cfrac{\Sigma \, (Y-\overline{Y})^2 (1-N^2)}{(N-2)} \left[\cfrac{1}{N} + \cfrac{\overline{X^2}}{\Sigma \, (X-\overline{X})^2} \right]}}$$

presented in Table 21.) While this close correspondence was very desirable for the research, the distribution of intelligence introduced a problem when an attempt was made to assess the advantage of a head start in reading, in relation to the intelligence of the 30 early readers in the special experimental group.

Table 21. Distribution of IQ scores in the total group of 156 early readers, and in the selected group of 30 early readers

IQ Range	156 Early Readers		30 Early Readers	
	NUMBER	PER CENT	NUMBER	PER CENT
80— 89	1	.6	0	.0
90— 99	5	3.2	1	3.3
100—109	5	3.2	1	3.3
110—119	23	14.7	3	10.0
120—129	26	16.7	7	23.3
130—139	47	30.1	9	30.0
140—149	37	23.7	6	20.0
150—159	9	5.8	2	6.7
160—169	2	1.3	0	.0
170—179	1	.6	1	3.3

In the California study, it will be recalled, reading achievement and intelligence data suggested a special advantage for the early readers with the lower IQ's (see Tables 10, 12, and 14). However, IQ scores in the California research, in contrast to those in the New York study, were more equally distributed over the obtained IQ range. Because of the uneven distribution of intelligence levels in the New York study, a division of the subjects in the special experimental group on the basis of IQ scores would result in very small numbers of subjects at certain IQ levels. Consequently, in the New York study the relationship between the intelligence of the early reader and the advantage of his head start was examined by dividing the 30 early readers into three groups of equal size. The IQ ranges resulting from this numerical division of subjects are shown in Table 22. The second column in the table (the median IQ's) also shows that the information pertains to bright children. Possible reactions to the brightness of these 30 early readers are multiple; two very different kinds will be mentioned here.

The first reaction would be a kind of protest. It would voice the complaint that the early reader and the non-early-reader comparisons in the New York study are of limited value and application because of their concentration on two groups of bright children. A second and a very different kind of possible reaction should also be noted, however. This reaction might be summarized as follows. Data in the California study suggested that a head start in reading is of special advantage for

Table 22. Advantage of a head start in reading in relation to intelligence

Intelligence Quotient		Number of Early Readers	Mean Difference Scores, in Years		
RANGE	MEDIAN		MAY 1962	MAY 1963	MAY 1964
99—124	119.5	10	+0.52 [a]	+0.61	+0.98
126—134	132.5	10	+1.02	+1.03	+0.90
135—170	146.5	10	+1.46	+1.21	+1.14

[a] Positive difference scores indicate early readers showed higher achievement than the non-early-readers with whom they were paired.

the less bright child. Therefore, in concentrating on groups of bright children in the New York phase of the research, the possible value of a head start is perhaps being assessed unfairly—in the sense that it is probably *under*estimated.

Other reactions to the data presented in Table 22 are possible; but the explication of these two is enough to demonstrate that the same data can elicit very diverse reactions, and even diverse kinds of complaints.

With this in mind, two observations concerning these data are noteworthy. The first is about the difference scores, examined one year at a time. Looked at in this way, difference scores indicate that, among bright children, the higher the IQ, the greater is the advantage of earlier reading. The second observation is about the same data when they are examined over a three-year period. Looked at over time, the data indicate that the advantage of a head start is increasing for the less bright, but decreasing for the brightest children.

This trend of the data, over time, suggested to this researcher the possibility, and the possible value, of comparing the reading achievement of all the 125 early readers who remained in New York City public schools for the duration of the reseach with the reading achievement of their classmates. Procedures for making the comparison could have duplicated those used in the California achievement comparisons. Unfortunately—at least for this research—it was subsequently learned that the New York City public schools had discontinued the use of group intelligence tests, primarily because of their middle-class orientation [15]. As a result, nothing else was done in this second study to try to assess the advantage of a head start in reading, in relation to the intelligence of the early reader.

Chapter **VIII**

Family Interviews in the Second Study

Interviews in the second study were held with families of the 30 early readers in the special experimental group, and with families of the 30 non-early-readers comprising the control group. As in the first study, this interviewing was done during the initial year of the research.

In New York, with the approval of school personnel, this writer made the contacts with families—initially by mail and then by phone—to explain the reason for the interviews, to get permission to go to the homes, and to arrange for specific appointments. To parents of both early readers and non-early-readers, the explanation given for the interviews was this writer's interest in improving the early years of schooling—improvement which depended upon increased knowledge about the preschool years of children. It was on these preschool years, parents were told, that the interview questions would focus.

Reactions to the request for an interview varied. During the phone conversations, some parents agreed immediately while others consented only after much questioning. Some parents said they would have to contact school principals before agreeing to an interview. Others said they would "have to think about it," and requested a second phone call. Still other parents asked for this researcher's office phone number, saying they would return the call. (Later, in an interview, one mother said she had asked for the office phone number to find out whether the caller really was a professor.)

While there was this variation in initial responses to the request for home interviews, all 60 of the families consented. In the interviews themselves the parents were cooperative and, generally, cordial—even the

87

mother who carried on the beginning of the interview in the hallway of her apartment building. Later, inside the apartment, she explained that she had to make certain the interviewer was a professor, not a seller of encyclopedias. (This parent said she had mentioned the interview to a neighbor who told her "to watch out" because "salesmen use any trick to get their foot in the door.")

The Interview Questionnaire

What was learned in the California study about the preschool years of early readers had raised many questions that were left without answers. One result of these unanswered questions was a new questionnaire that was longer than the one used in the first study. Fortunately, its initial form was tried out with six parents not connected with the New York research. These trial interviews clearly demonstrated that the questionnaire was sufficiently lengthy that it became a source of fatigue and boredom for the interviewee, and even for the interviewer.

To shorten interviewing time, three procedures were followed to alter the questionnaire. The first was to delete questions judged not to be of central importance to the research. These included queries about the frequency with which parents visited their child's school, and about the parents' best and worst subjects when they themselves were students.

The second procedure for shortening the questionnaire was to omit questions which were not necessarily basic to the research and which, in the six trial interviews, consistently elicited responses that seemed stereotyped and devoid of individuality. For instance, one question in the trial interviews asked whether parents had any special hopes or ambitions for their children. To the question, all six parents responded by saying they just wanted their children to be happy adults. Because further informal probing resulted in the same response, this question was deleted. Other questions judged to be of a kind that fosters stereotyped answers included: "What do you feel are the most important characteristics or traits for a child to learn?" ("How to get along with other people") and "What kinds of grades do you think your child should get as he goes through school?" ("What's important is that he does his best").

The third procedure for shortening interview time in the New York research was used with greater frequency. This procedure appended categories of possible responses to most of the questions on the questionnaire form. These allowed the interviewer to record a response merely by checking one or more categories. In most instances, the content of the response categories was suggested by interview data from the California research. In other instances, the content was either the logical or the only possibilities.

It should be pointed out that these categories of responses in the New York questionnaire were not used to prompt particular kinds of answers. Parents still responded freely to a given question. If the content of their response matched the content of a category, that category was checked. If a parent's response was not included in available categories, then the response was written by the interviewer.

In the New York research, the same questionnaire was used with parents of early readers and with the parents of non-early-readers. However, not all questions were pertinent for all non-early-readers. For instance, when the parent of a non-early-reader said her child showed no preschool interest in learning to read, then two questions were not relevant—one about the age of the child when initial interest in reading was shown, and the one about possible sources of the early interest.

For the most part, the basic content of the New York questions duplicated the content of questions used in the California study. Some questions were added, of course, because of what was learned in the first study. These were such inquiries as: "When no other children were available, what did your child usually do to occupy his time?" "Did your child like to play alone?" "Did your child watch any nursery-school–kindergarten-type programs on television?"

Like the California questionnaire, the one used in New York made no attempt to study the psychological dimensions of family life. Again, the omission results from this writer's conviction that such obviously relevant factors as the pressures put upon children by their parents—and especially the more subtle ones—cannot be identified by means of an interview.

The final version of the interview questionnaire is presented as Appendix C.

Interviews and Interviewees

Interview procedures in New York paralleled those used in the first study. For instance, an effort was made to hold interviews during the hours when school was in session. With five exceptions, adherence to this time schedule was possible. Working mothers made it necessary to hold three Saturday morning interviews, and two evening interviews.

Although the choice of daytime interviewing hours reduced the number of fathers who were likely to be present, an overwhelming impression left by all 60 of the New York home visits was that even if the researcher had said, "I can come to your home at any time on any day," there would still have been very few interviews for which the father was present. Over and over again fathers were described as being on the road most of the time; as working during the day and going to school at night; as spending long hours at the office; as having two jobs. The experience of doing the interviewing certainly brought to mind "the vanishing American father" referred to in so many titles of popular magazine articles.

As a summary, the following numerical distribution of interviewees in the New York study is presented:

Early Readers		Non-Early-Readers	
Mother	27	Mother	28
Mother and father	1	Mother and father	2
Mother and grandmother	1		
Grandmother	1		

For all but 3 interviews about the early readers, the mother alone was present. The one father who was interviewed was a lawyer; he explained his presence by saying, "I can usually manage to set up my own working hours." In another case, the maternal grandmother was present because she lived with the family. In another instance, the early reader was an illegitimate child who was being raised by grandparents.[1] One early reader's father was deceased, and in three cases the parents were divorced.

For the non-early-readers there were two interviews for which both the mother and the father were present. Interestingly, one of these fathers also was a lawyer. The other was a fireman. In the case of the 28 interviews for which only the mother was present, one father was deceased and in another case the parents were divorced.

The Sixty Subjects and Their Families

To provide a framework for the comparison data to be reported later in this chapter, certain information generally descriptive of the subjects and their families is presented here. The source of the information is interview data.

It will be recalled that the selection of a control group was accomplished by pairing 30 non-early-readers with 30 of the 156 early readers (19 boys and 11 girls) on the bases of intelligence, sex, and first-grade teacher. In this control group, 29 of the children were Caucasian and the other was Oriental. Comprising the group of 30 early readers were 28 Caucasians and 2 Negroes.

To identify the socioeconomic status of the 60 families being interviewed, the factors of parent education, occupation, source of income, and house type were considered.[2] Information about these four variables was converted into socioeconomic levels according to Warner's Index of Social Class [98]. A summary of the results appears in Table 23.

In interpreting the data in Table 23, it is important to keep in mind that members of the total group of first-graders ($N = 4,465$) from which

[1] In the report of data, these grandparents are treated as parents.
[2] In assessing the socioeconomic backgrounds of early readers in the California study, the factor of dwelling area was also considered. This variable was not used in the New York study because in a borough such as Manhattan it is common to find a luxurious apartment building only one block away from a row of slum dwellings.

Table 23. Percentage of 30 early readers and of 30 non-early-readers
in each of five socioeconomic classes

| Subjects | Socioeconomic Status | | | | |
	LOWER-LOWER	UPPER-LOWER	LOWER-MIDDLE	UPPER-MIDDLE	LOWER-UPPER
Early readers	3.3	23.3	33.3	33.3	6.7
Non-early-readers	—	20.0	40.0	13.3	26.7

the New York early readers were identified might not have been equally
distributed among the various socioeconomic classes. As was explained
in Chapter VI, the attempt was made to choose New York City schools
which, together, would represent fairly equally all of the socioeconomic
levels—with the exception, of course, of the upper-upper class which
would not be included in a public school population. To what exact degree this attempt was successful is not known; but it is believed that the
total group was at least not markedly skewed.

A second point to remember is that lower-class communities in New
York City have a high proportion of Puerto Ricans. This fact is relevant
to the study being reported because the bilingualism of Puerto Rican
children is not likely to be associated with preschool ability in the reading of English.

Actually, when the New York home interviews were completed, it
was found that none of the 30 early readers, but 4 children among the
group of 30 non-early-readers, came from bilingual families. In each instance of bilingualism, a different second language was spoken. More
specifically, Italian, German, French, and Chinese were the second languages. In the case of the Oriental family, the mother said all members
spoke Chinese at home, but the children "sprinkled their Chinese with
English words." In many instances, for both the early readers and the
non-early-readers, parents referred to their children's knowledge of
Yiddish expressions. This would be expected because 21 children in the
group of 30 early readers, and 22 children among the 30 non-early-
readers, were Jewish.

A third point to keep in mind in interpreting the socioeconomic data
in Table 23 is the fact that in the wealthiest of the 60 families interviewed, the children were cared for by maids. In general, these maids
were young women who, it was reported, remained with a family for
about a year. Generally, too, as described by parents, the maids had no
special training—nor even, sometimes, a high school diploma. All of this
is to say that this writer's initial assumption about the special care given
to children of wealth turned out to be somewhat naïve. In fact, a few
of the New York interviews clearly defined the meaning of the term
"poor little rich child."

A few other pieces of information about the 60 subjects and their families will add substance to the framework for thinking about certain differences, reported in the next section, between the early readers and the non-early-readers.

The chronological ages of the two groups were very similar. At their entrance into first grade, the median age of the early readers was 6.3 years; and their ages ranged from 5.9 years to 6.8 years. For the non-early-readers, the median chronological age at the start of first grade was 6.4 years, and the range was from 5.9 years up to 6.7 years.

Interview questions also asked about the age when subjects began to walk and to talk. By age one, 29 of the early readers and 24 of the non-early-readers were able to walk. At the same age, according to the parents, 16 of the early readers and 13 of the non-early-readers were talking.

Interview data about handedness were interesting: 8 of the early readers and 8 of the non-early-readers were left-handed; none were ambidextrous.

Other interview data indicated that all 30 of the non-early-readers attended kindergarten for a year. All but one of the early readers also had been to kindergarten. Among the early readers, 13 went to nursery school; of the non-early-readers, 9 attended nursery school.

Of particular interest to this researcher was the makeup of the 60 families, especially because of the pronounced influence of sibling help reported in the California research. Presented below is a description of family size:

	Number of children in family, including subject:				
	1	2	3	4	5
Number of early readers	8	16	4	2	0
Number of non-early-readers	2	16	10	1	1

This summary shows larger families among the non-early-readers. For this research, however, family size cannot be isolated from information about age differences among the children in a family—especially the differences in age between a subject and older siblings. Information about these age differences is summarized below:

	Age difference, in years, between subject and next older sibling:													
	1	2	3	4	5	6	7	8	9	10	11	12	13	14
Number of early readers	1	2	5	2	1	0	0	1	1	0	0	1	0	0
Number of non-early-readers	0	2	4	2	2	4	2	0	2	0	0	0	0	1

This summary shows that 14 of the early readers and 19 of the non-early readers had at least one older sibling. However, the summary also indicates that age differences between a subject and the next oldest child in his family tended to be greater for non-early-readers than for early readers. This finding will be commented upon in a later section of the chapter.

Reporting the Main Comparison Data

One major reason for doing this second study was to compare the preschool years of early readers and non-early-readers. The procedure used to collect information was parent interviews. Any comparison, of course, reveals both likenesses and differences. However, the following three sections of this chapter, reporting the interview responses considered most useful as providing the data for this comparison, will focus mainly on differences. For those interested, the entire comparison of interview responses can be found in Appendix C.

In concentrating on differences, an immediate concern is the question of what constitutes a difference sufficient to merit explicit and serious attention. For this research the decision was to note any difference of 20 per cent or more between the response frequencies for the two groups of interviewees.[3] For instance, since 25 of the mothers of the 30 early readers (83 per cent) and 10 of the mothers of the 30 non-early-readers (33 per cent) described themselves as reading more often than the average adult, this difference is made explicit in this chapter and reported as: *More mothers of early readers said they read more often than the average adult* (83—33). And since 9 of the mothers of the 30 early readers (30 per cent) and 21 of the mothers of the 30 non-early-readers (70 per cent) believed that reading ought to be taught by a trained person, this difference is also mentioned, and reported as: *Fewer mothers of early readers believed that reading ought to be taught by a trained person* (30—70).

The decision to call attention to differences of 20 per cent or more was arbitrary. It was felt that such differences were large enough to warrant attention in this research and also, perhaps, a more precise and statistical evaluation in future research. Until such research is done, the differences to be discussed in this chapter can be used only to contrast the 30 early readers and the 30 non-early-readers in this New York study.

In reporting these differences in parents' responses, there is no presumption of accuracy for individual responses. Indeed, the experience of doing interviews for the two studies resulted in an intensification of this writer's consciousness of the great differences among parents—including differences in their awareness of what their children did and

[3] A percentage difference was selected because certain interview questions were not asked of all parents of the non-early-readers.

did not do, of what they did and did not like, and even of the kinds of human beings they were. The suspicion also grew, as more and more interviews were completed, that parental attitudes and values affect responses even to questions which, basically, are factual in nature. For example, a parent who suspects television should be viewed as lowbrow entertainment might respond with less than perfect accuracy to a question that asks about the number of hours her child spends watching television. Or, to cite another illustration, a parent who is asked why she offered no assistance to a preschool child who seemed interested in learning to read might tend to respond with a rationalization rather than an explanation.

These few comments simply say—again—that the data in this chapter reflect what parents were both willing and able to report in home interviews.

Differences for Questions Asked in All Sixty Interviews

More mothers of early readers were college graduates (33—10).

The difference noted above is of interest, especially when two other factors are considered: (1) In the California study, concern about problems ensuing from early reading was associated with higher levels of education; and (2) In the New York research, it was mothers who provided most of the help that led to preschool achievement in reading. Does this combination of facts suggest a change in the attitude of the more highly educated mother toward preschool reading?

Obviously, the small number of subjects in the two studies reported here hardly allows for a revelation of new facts applicable to all parents. However, neither the small number of subjects nor any of the findings about them and their parents preclude the possibility that there really was a change in the attitude of the more highly educated parent, between 1958 and 1961.

The existence of this possibility prompts inquiry about why such a change might have occurred. Two reasons are suggested here. The first is the likelihood that, in 1961, schools were saying much less, if anything, about the inadvisability of parents' helping preschool children with beginning learnings in skills such as reading.[4] A second reason is rooted in the change to be found, in 1961, in the general thinking about the potential of young children—a difference described in Chapter VI. Published accounts of some of the more optimistic opinions about this potential probably were (and are) read more frequently by mothers

---

[4] It was interesting to note that New York parents who did mention a teacher's opposition to preschool reading help generally referred to a teacher who had taught an older child in the family.

with more years of formal education. If so, this might help to explain the more positive attitude of the New York college-educated mothers toward preschool reading.

The difference in the educational backgrounds of the mothers of the 30 early readers and the mothers of the 30 non-early-readers in the New York study may contribute to the next difference to be reported:

More mothers of early readers said they read more often than the average adult (83—33).[5]

This kind of difference again emphasizes the likelihood of an early reader having in his home an adult model who reads often. Perhaps, like other attitudes, early interest in becoming a reader is as much "caught" as it is taught.

It is logical to assume that another way in which a child "catches" early interest in reading is by being read to. Consequently, parents were asked in the interviews: *Did you or anybody else read to _____ before he started school?* Responses showed the following difference:

More early readers were read to at home, prior to entering school (100—73).

Another question, presented only to the parents who said their preschool children had been read to, asked how the reading had been done. In response, all of these parents said no one particular pattern was used. However, the following procedures were mentioned in the frequencies indicated:

Procedures in Home Reading	Early Readers	Non-Early-Readers
Identified words when children asked about them	80%	41%
Talked about pictures	73	68
Pointed to words as they were being read	40	32
Asked children questions about story content	17	36

Other questions in the New York interviews asked for opinions about the teaching of reading. Responses showed the following differences:

Fewer mothers of early readers believed that reading ought to be taught by a trained person (30—70).

More mothers of early readers said parents should give help with skills like reading to preschool children (100—50).

[5] The definition of reading for the "average adult" was the same as that used in the California interviews.

The relevance to this research of the two differences cited above is so obvious that comments are unnecessary. However, it is important to be explicit about the additional fact that 25 of the 30 mothers of early readers conditioned their endorsement of parental help with reading by adding, "If the children are interested." In the case of the mothers of non-early-readers, 13 of the 15 who did not disapprove of early help also referred to the relevance of the child's interest. It is this awareness of the importance of the learner's own interest which probably accounts for the fact that a parent could maintain that reading ought to be taught by a trained person, but at the same time approve of preschool parental help with reading skills.

As can be seen in the two differences noted above, 50 per cent of the mothers of the 30 non-early-readers did not approve of such help. The most frequent reason given for this was the belief that preschool help would lead to problems of confusion when the children started school. Asked about the source of this belief, 11 of these 15 mothers recalled the past warnings of teachers of older children in the family.

Among the parents of the 30 early readers—all of whom were aware of their children's preschool achievement in reading—5 expressed concern about the early learning. In each instance, the concern was explained by reference to the possibility that the early achievement would lessen a child's interest in school. Since the interviewing was done during the year the early readers were in first grade, it is possible that this particular concern reflected a description of what was, rather than a prediction of what might happen.

Because of the amount of play in a young child's life, some of the questions in the New York interviews focused on preschool play activities. Certain differences between the early readers and the non-early-readers were found. For instance, when parents were asked about the types of play activities in which their children did especially well, the following difference was noted:

More early readers were described as being adept in activities that could be characterized as "quiet" (63—37).[6]

When parents were asked how the children had spent their time when playmates were unavailable, this difference showed up:

Fewer early readers played with toys (7—40).

Responses to a question about typical play activities when other children were available revealed the following difference:

[6] Questions about play activities could have many different answers. To see the possible significance of the differences reported in this chapter, information about all of the responses should be examined. This information can be found in Appendix C.

More early readers, when playing with other children, participated in quiet games (70—43).

As was mentioned earlier, the three differences in play activities which have just been cited are based on responses to questions for which many different answers were possible. However, one question about pre-school play had a Yes–No answer. This question asked, *Did your child like to play alone?* According to the parents, this difference existed:

More early readers liked to play alone (80—37).

Parents' subsequent comments about their responses to this question indicated that "liking to play alone" can mean different things for different children. A sampling of some of the parents' comments is given below:

He had to learn to like playing alone. There weren't any children around, and I couldn't take him to the park every day.

She was always an independent child. She's not one who would ask, "What should I do?"

It's hard to describe her. She liked to play with other children and would run wild with them. Yet she could spend hours playing by herself in the house.

He seemed perfectly content, talking to himself and playing with his books.

She always liked to write with pencils. But her father's an architect, and that's probably why.

She liked to play alone, but she liked it better when I'd play with her.

He was three when his brother was born. From that time on, it seemed, he didn't want to go outside. He spent most of the time, indoors, watching TV, coloring, playing at his blackboard, and with his books.

He liked to play alone before he went to school. School made him more gregarious.

Because television was one of the sources of interest which led to the early reading described in the California study, five questions in the New York interviews focused on the television habits of the early readers and the non-early-readers. From these questions, three differences between the groups will be noted.

The first difference indicated that the early readers spent less time watching television, prior to entering kindergarten. This difference is stated below in the form used to report other differences in this chapter:

In a week's time, fewer early readers watched television for six hours or more (70—93).

More descriptive than the statement above, however, is a summary of parents' reports about the frequency with which their children watched television before entering school. The summary follows:

Number of Hours Per Week	Number of Early Readers [7]	Number of Non-Early-Readers
5 or less	8	2
6—10	9	11
11—15	7	7
16—20	4	4
21—25	1	3
25 or more	0	3

Two comments should be made about these data. The first is a repetition of a fact reported earlier; namely, that more of the early readers attended nursery school, which in turn reduced the number of daytime hours spent at home—and, possibly, the amount of time spent in watching television. The second comment could be made about any of the interview data, for it is the reminder that information regarding the television habits of the 60 subjects was based on what parents were both able and willing to report.

What parents were able and willing to report also identified differences concerned with "valuable learnings" resulting from watching television.[8] One such difference (very closely related to the concern of the research) is large enough to be described in this chapter:

As a result of watching television, more early readers developed a curiosity about written words (53—10).

Another interview question asked parents whether the subjects had watched any TV programs of the nursery-school–kindergarten type. Responses identified the following difference:

Fewer early readers watched programs of the nursery-school–kindergarten type (60—80).

In a sense, this difference is unexpected; but two other factors— both mentioned earlier in the chapter—could suggest at least a partial explanation. One is the fact that 13 of the early readers but only 9 of the non-early-readers attended nursery school. Because the hours of

---

[7] The family of one early reader did not have a television set.

[8] "Valuable learnings" were defined as "any learning that might help a child in school."

nursery school probably coincided with the scheduled times of the school-like television programs, fewer early readers would be at home to watch the programs. The other relevant factor, of course, is that the early readers, as a group, were reported to have watched television less often than the non-early-readers.

As it turned out, the difference between the two groups of children in relation to the watching of school-like programs on television had little pertinence for this research. Surprisingly, none of these programs ever were mentioned by parents as influencing their children's early interest in learning to read. Television commercials, quiz programs, and weather reports were considered much more important, both as sources of interest in reading and, later, as reading materials. Actually, some parents were critical of the more school-like programs because the "teachers" so persistently urged children to buy—as one mother said—"this, that, and the other thing." In another interview a mother commented, "Those programs certainly caused a lot of arguments in this house. You couldn't possibly buy all those things."

Another series of questions in the New York interviews focused on the subjects' experiences in first grade. It was while the children were enrolled in first grade, it will be recalled, that the interviewing was done. From the questions about first grade, the only finding that merits attention in this chapter is the following:

Fewer early readers were described as being interested in first grade (60—87).

Two comments seem appropriate here. The first is the observation that most first-grade reading programs are built on the assumption that beginning first graders cannot read. Consequently, unless teachers are able to individualize instruction, early readers will often be taught what they already know, especially in the beginning months of the school year. This particular observation was summarized most succinctly by a New York early reader who said of her first-grade experiences, "I already know what the teacher keeps telling us."

The second comment to be made about the subjects' interest in first grade is related to another interview finding:

Fewer parents of the early readers expressed satisfaction with the way the schools teach reading (53—73).

This finding about parental attitudes toward school efforts to teach reading certainly could be related to the previously mentioned finding about the subjects' interest in first grade. At least it is valid to ask whether parental opinions about reading instruction might not affect their perceptions of the children's interest in first grade. On the other hand, it is not unreasonable to wonder whether a child's interest in first grade might not affect his parent's view of how successful and appropriate the school instruction is.

The next difference to be reported is directly related to the major concern of the research. This difference was identified by an interview question which asked, *Did your child show any preschool interest in learning to read?* Parents' responses are summarized below:

More early readers showed preschool interest in learning to read (100—73).

Differences in Preschool
Interest in Reading

Whenever a parent said her child showed early interest in reading, two other questions about the early interest were asked. One question inquired about its possible sources; the other asked about the age of the child when the interest became apparent.

When responses about the sources of a child's early interest were examined, it was found that parents of the early readers mentioned more kinds; and, as a group, they mentioned them with greater frequency. The important differences between the two groups with respect to sources of interest are summarized below:

More parents of early readers attributed preschool interest in reading partly to . . .
   . . . availability of paper and pencils in the home (83—18).
   . . . availability of reading materials in the home (73—14).
   . . . availability of a blackboard in the home (57—23).
   . . . interest in the meaning of words (47—9).

The interview question which asked parents about the age of their children when preschool interest in reading first developed elicited the following information:

Age of Initial Interest	Early Readers (N=30)	Non-Early-Readers (N=22)
Less than 3	17%	9%
3	33	32
4	50	41
5	0	18

As in the first study (see Table 6), the age of four is still the age most commonly associated with the start of an early interest in becoming a reader.

Differences in Preschool
Help with Reading

Findings reported in the previous section centered on 30 early readers (100 per cent of the early readers) and on 22 non-early-readers (73 per cent of the non-early-readers) who showed preschool interest in learning to read. Subsequent to the interview question which asked parents about the age of the children when the interest in reading became known, another question was posed: *At what age did you or anybody else begin to give _____ help with reading?* For the 30 early readers and 15 of the 22 non-early-readers, responses indicated that the age at which help was started coincided with the age of the child when the interest was expressed. This correspondence would be expected, if only because age was being described in years, a large unit when young children are the subjects.

But what about the other 7 non-early-readers who were described as having shown early interest in reading? In interviews, they were reported to have received no preschool help either with reading or with related skills such as spelling and printing. Parents' explanations for the lack of help referred to (1) teachers of older children in the family who, in prior years, warned parents not to teach preschool children to read; (2) possible problems of confusion or boredom when the children would be in first grade; and (3) insufficient time to give help.[9]

Once it was established that subjects did receive preschool help with reading (30 early readers and 15 non-early-readers), seven kinds of possible help were mentioned, one at a time, to their parents. The parents were asked whether they or anybody else had given each kind of help. Two of the seven questions got very similar responses from the two groups of parents: 100 per cent of both early readers and non-early-readers received preschool help with *identification of letters;* 93 per cent of the early readers, and 87 per cent of the non-early-readers, were helped with *identification of numbers.* For the other five kinds of help, there were considerable differences between the responses for the two groups:

More parents of early readers gave preschool help with . . .
    . . . *printing* (93—73).
    . . . *identification of written words* (91—27).
    . . . *the meaning of words* (77—27).
    . . . *spelling* (73—27).
    . . . *the sounds of letters* (67—27).

[9] Immediately following each family interview, the interviewer wrote a spontaneous and impressionistic reaction report. Now, when the 60 reactions are reviewed, a pronounced difference between the two groups of parents is seen: the mothers of the non-early-readers more often characterized themselves as being busy. What is interesting is that the factual circumstances of the "busy" mothers—at least the circumstances discussed in interviews—did not always suggest that their family responsibilities were greater than those of the mothers of the early readers.

At this point it is time to ask why the children were given preschool help. When parents were asked about the reasons, these were their responses:

Reasons for Preschool Help with Language Skills	Early Readers (N=30)	Non-Early-Readers (N=15)
To answer children's questions and requests for help	83%	67%
To keep the children occupied	47	33
To teach the children to read	13	7

One other question was asked of parents who indicated that preschool help with reading and related skills had been given. This question inquired, *Who were the people who gave _____ most of the preschool help with things like the identification of numbers and letters and words, or with printing and spelling, and so on?* The parents' responses are summarized below:

Most Influential Persons	Early Readers (N=30)	Non-Early-Readers (N=15)
Mother	93%	87%
Sister	13	27
Other relative	10	7
Brother	7	0
Father	3	13

To compare these findings about 30 New York early readers with the findings about the 49 early readers in California, the following data are presented:

Most Influential Persons	New York Early Readers	California Early Readers
Mother	93%	59%
Sibling	20	53
Other relative	10	4
Father	3	14

A very noticeable trend in these two sets of data is the greater influence of mothers and the lesser influence of siblings in the New York study. Logically, a combination of facts could account for both differences: (1) Older siblings were present in the families of 82 per cent of the early readers in California, and in the families of only 54 per cent of the 30 New York early readers. (2) The age difference between an early reader and the next oldest child in his family tended to be smaller in the California study. (3) In California, more of the next oldest children were girls.[10]

---

[10] This concentration on the makeup of families is not designed to overshadow the possibility that a change in parental attitude toward preschool help with reading might also be a factor contributing to the greater influence of mothers in the New York study.

These three facts have been pointed out here, not only to offer a possible explanation for the lesser influence of sibling help in the New York phase of the research, but, in addition, to serve as a reminder that there are no simple, single answers to such questions as: How significant to preschool reading is the factor of sibling help? The same reminder, stated in more general terms, would suggest that the more a topic is researched, the clearer it becomes that there are neither simple questions nor simple answers.

Personality Characteristics of the Early Readers and the Non-Early-Readers

In the final part of each New York interview, two procedures were used to collect information about the parent's view of the child's personality. The first procedure comprised the asking of three questions:

1. During this interview you have used many different words to describe your child. Now I'd like to try to get a total picture of him. Could you tell me again the words that best describe your child?

2. If somebody else were to take care of your child, what would you feel was especially important for her to know about him?

3. Does your child have any characteristics which he showed as an infant, and which he still shows?

Some comments will be made about the research value of these questions before the responses are reported.

The first question seemed successful in eliciting personality descriptions. Once, though, an unexpected answer was given and the question was repeated. The unexpected response was that of an older mother who had one child. The mother said of this child, "All she wants, all she talks about is a baby brother or sister." The mother then went on to tell about the little girl's great disappointment when her father returned home from the hospital, following a gall bladder operation, without a baby!

The second question was much less successful in eliciting answers which pertained to personality. One trend in parents' responses showed frequent attention to physical factors and needs. The other trend consisted of two opposite reactions, both focusing on the "baby sitting" aspect of the question. On the one hand, certain mothers showed surprise that the interviewer would even suggest that other people took care of their children. On the other hand, however, there were responses typified by the answer of a mother who said of her son, "He's so accustomed to being cared for by others that there aren't any problems about it."

The third in the series of three questions also was minimally successful in identifying personality traits. Most often, parents' responses dealt with physical factors related to sleeping and eating habits. Once, though, in answer to the third question, a mother of an early reader commented, "Right from the start he was a persistent, determined child. In fact, his father often remarked that if he had been the first child, he'd also be the last one."

Actually, this parent's comment provides an excellent introduction to a summary report of personality traits as described by parents in New York interviews, because it suggests that descriptions such as "persistent" —or "affectionate" or "neat"—probably characterize a child in relation to others in his family, or even to individuals outside the family group. For example, in the case of the boy mentioned above, the two older sons in the family might also be persistent, but compared to this youngest boy they might be viewed as very docile children.

Table 24. Descriptions of 30 early readers and 30 non-early-readers given by parents in interviews

Trait	Number of Early Readers	Number of Non-Early-Readers
Intelligent	14	9
Curious	10	9
Persistent; determined	9	11
Friendly; outgoing	8	3
Sensitive; feelings easily hurt	8	6
Energetic; active	7	5
Serious	7	2
Aggressive; forward	6	3
Competitive	5	1
Happy	5	0
Affectionate	4	2
Good disposition	4	3
Needs to be praised	4	5
High-strung	3	1
Neat	3	0
Quiet	3	2
Generous	2	1
Good memory	2	0
Good sense of humor	2	3
Shy	2	0
Worrier	2	1
Eager to please adults	1	0
Eager to keep up with older sibling	1	0
Imaginative	1	3
Independent	1	5
Perfectionistic	1	1
Temperamental; moody	1	0
Artistic	0	1
A leader	0	1
Totals	116	78

The comparative aspect of parents' responses to the three questions about personality should be kept in mind in examining the summary of interview data presented in Table 24. For this summary, identical responses to the three different questions were counted as having been given only once. Too, whenever terms were considered to be synonymous ("persistent" and "determined"), both terms were listed but they were counted as one response. And, finally, whenever the equivalence of different terms was questionable ("competitive" and "eager to keep up with older sibling"), the terms were assumed to refer to different traits and were listed separately.

Probably the most interesting feature of the data presented in Table 24 is the close similarity of the two groups of children. For instance, the greatest frequency difference is only 5; this is for the descriptions "intelligent," "friendly," "serious," and "happy"—all more often applied to early readers. Here, though, a question must be raised about the meaning of the frequency differences. It may be that more early readers did possess these traits; but it is also possible that the differences reflect the greater fluency of the parents of the early readers. As Table 24 presents the data, a total of 116 responses were given by parents of early readers, while only 78 were given by the parents of the non-early-readers.

Another procedure used in the New York interviews to learn more about the subjects focused on five selected characteristics. Criteria for selecting these characteristics came from the California interview data. *Persistent* and *perfectionistic* were chosen because they were cited most frequently by the parents of California early readers, when direct questions about the characteristics of the children were asked (see page 50). *Competitive, curious,* and *good memory* were the terms most often used in the California interviews as the parents responded to the many questions which did not deal explicitly with the predominant characteristics of their children.

For each New York interview the five characteristics were listed on a sheet of paper, randomly arranged as follows:

_____ good memory
_____ persistent
_____ curious
_____ competitive
_____ perfectionistic

Giving the parent the sheet, the interviewer said: "I have a list of words which might or might not describe your child. If a word does describe him accurately, would you put a check in front of it? If a word does not describe your child, leave the space blank."

Once a parent had followed these directions, the interviewer said: "Would you look over the list again? If there is any word in the list which is an absolutely perfect description of your child, would you put a double check in front of that word?"

How parents responded to these requests is summarized below: [11]

	Very Descriptive (Double-checked)	Descriptive (Checked once)	Not Descriptive (Not checked)
GOOD MEMORY			
Early readers	21	7	2
Non-early-readers	21	8	1
PERSISTENT			
Early readers	16	14	0
Non-early-readers	13	13	4
CURIOUS			
Early readers	25	5	0
Non-early-readers	25	5	0
COMPETITIVE			
Early readers	19	8	3
Non-early-readers	13	10	7
PERFECTIONISTIC			
Early readers	9	11	10
Non-early-readers	8	12	10

In this distribution, the greatest difference to be found between early readers and non-early-readers is in the responses to *competitive*.[12] But even for this trait, the distribution of the 60 responses could be the result of chance. Consequently, the only possible conclusion is one arrived at earlier: the early readers and the 30 non-early-readers were very similar, as described by their parents in interviews.

Impressions from the New York Interviews

Some researchers would claim that impressions resulting from interviews merit no space in a research report. Impressions, they would say, are so subjective and, possibly, so biased that they are of meager help in efforts to identify facts and valid generalizations.

Prior to the studies described in this report, prompt support for the claim of these researchers would have come from this writer. Now, however, the support wavers. Now, six years and two studies later, this writer has a somewhat different view of interview data. Part of this view is the uneasy feeling that even data which appear to be "objective" and

[11] The following example shows how the summary is to be interpreted. Of the 30 parents of early readers, a total of 28 checked *good memory* and 2 did not. Of the 28 who checked this trait the first time, 21 checked it again the second time (double-checked it) and 7 left it single-checked.

[12] It is interesting to note the differences between these descriptions of the 60 subjects and the descriptions that resulted from the three openended interview questions (see Table 24). This researcher cannot account for the differences—and certainly cannot make a judgment about which data are more valid. However, the differences do serve as a reminder that personality data collected in varying ways can lead to very different findings.

"scientific" are subject to interpretation—and thus to misinterpretation. The problem of identical words having different meanings for different people and the fact that the interview response of each person derives from a frame of reference which is uniquely his own are just two of the many reasons for remembering that objective data are not necessarily self-explanatory.

Another by-product of the experience of doing these two studies is an awareness that some of the most interesting and, perhaps, some of the most relevant information in an interview comes not from prescribed and carefully phrased questions but, rather, from the spontaneous comments and digressions of the interviewee. Of course, this particular observation could suggest that the wrong questions were asked in the interviews for this research. But the questions have been asked and answered, and the data they yielded have been reported. Now this writer would like to describe what might be called the marginal comments on interview questionnaires.

Immediately following each New York interview, this writer dictated what generally turned out to be two single-spaced, typewritten pages of reactions. To insure that the reaction reports would have at least a minimum of organization, three general categories were used for the content: (1) Subject, (2) Subject's Preschool Years, and (3) Parents. The categories were meant to be sufficiently broad that none would inhibit a free-flowing kind of commentary for the reaction reports.

Prior to the dictation of a report, each interview questionnaire was examined, question by question; but special attention went to the comments of an interviewee which were not directly elicited by a prescribed question. Direct quotes of interviewees were noted as often as they were available. The information gleaned from this systematic overview of questionnaire data, combined with the more subjective impressions of this writer, comprised the material for each reaction report.

When all 60 reports had been written, a research assistant studied them to identify pervasive similarities and differences between the early reader and the non-early-reader interviews. Meanwhile this writer re-read the two groups of reaction reports, for the same purpose. Later, a comparison was made between the two assessments. Points about which there was agreement were noted, and they will be discussed here. As a preface to this discussion, however, it must be emphasized that the element of independent agreement about trends in the reaction reports should not overshadow the fact that the reports themselves were only as valid as the impressions were accurate.

As the earlier discussions of interview data indicated, more of the early readers showed preschool curiosity about reading and related skills. What became evident in the reaction reports was the greater awareness of the early readers' parents about the details of the preschool curiosity. Yet, whenever parents either of early readers or of non-early-readers were able to describe the preschool interest with specific observations and illustrations, certain similarities became noticeable.

For example, with both groups of children alphabet books played an especially important role in stimulating early interest in letter names and, sometimes, in letter sounds. Also apparent was a similarity in the sequence with which interests and, in some instances, skills developed. Almost without exception the starting point of curiosity about written language was an interest in scribbling and drawing. From this developed interest in copying objects and letters of the alphabet. When a child was able to copy letters—and not all of the children who had the interest developed the skill—his almost inevitable request was, "Show me my name."

Many parents also told of how a child's interest in his own name grew to include interest in copying the names of parents and siblings, other relatives and friends, and sometimes pets. Here, too, it appeared that interest in copying led to long-term and, seemingly, intense "projects" which included, for example, the making and remaking of calendars and address books. What all of this emphasized is that preschool interest in reading very often develops from a prior interest in copying and writing. As one mother put it, some young children are "pencil and paper kids."

When children are "pencil and paper kids," one consequence is questions about the spelling of words. According to the reaction reports, the parents of the early readers and some of the parents of the non-early-readers provided answers to questions about spelling. Especially among the parents of the early readers, answers to these questions included intermittent discussions about the sounds of letters. The nature of these discussions could be characterized by the explanation of one early reader's mother, who said, "The help I gave with sounds was of the *bill–will–kill* variety." Why parents gave help with letter sounds is explained by another early reader's parent, who said of her daughter, "I didn't mind all of her questions about how do you spell this and how do you spell that, but I was hoping she'd learn to figure out some of the words by herself."

To be complete, this discussion of young children's interest in writing and spelling must be paired with a discussion of their question, "What does that word say?" From the reaction reports, two sources seemed especially important in stimulating queries about the identification of particular words. One source was the vast display of words found on signs, television commercials, calendars, cars and trucks, phonograph records, food packages, and the like. Here, the boys tended to learn words like *Chevrolet, stop,* and *train.* The girls, on the other hand, seemed especially attracted to words that were useful when they played house or played store. Often, these words were the names of foods.

The other source of curiosity about the identification of particular words was the experience of being read to. For this purpose, stories that were read and reread seemed more influential than those which were read only once or twice.

When parents commented about their children's request to have the same story read over and over again, they also tended to mention the ease with which the children memorized the stories. In one interview a mother said, "After a while I didn't know whether he enjoyed the story, or enjoyed telling me when it was time to turn the page."

It was during the interview discussions about these preschool years of the children that one very prominent difference between the parents of the early readers and the parents of the non-early-readers was identified. This difference pertained to opinions about the advisability of giving help to preschool children with skills like reading and writing. For the most part, parents of the early readers viewed the help they gave their children as a response to the children's questions. When these parents showed concern about the problems that could result, their worry was concentrated on the possibility of the children being bored in first grade.

In contrast to the interviews with the parents of early readers, those with the parents of the 30 non-early-readers were crowded with comments about the prospect of problems when parents give help with reading to preschool children. For example:

The system today is different. Reading is so important that it should be taught properly so that no complications arise.

I've always been told to let the school take care of the reading.

We have followed a strict "hands off" policy. . . . We have stayed out of forbidden territory.

When she asked about words, I just told her she'd learn to read when she got to first grade. . . . I didn't want to teach her anything that might cause problems later on.

I'm not an aggressive mother. Mine are normal, intelligent children. They'll learn in school. . . . I don't want to mix them up.

I believe the school should get it [reading] started. Then I'll help in whatever way I can.

In one non-early-reader interview, the lack of preschool help to a child interested in reading was explained by a mother who characterized herself with unusual candor:

I'm a driver, and I drove my first son into learning all kinds of things before he started school. . . . When he got there he didn't do very well. Sometimes, when I'd make him learn the words he'd say, "I hate you." I didn't want to have all that happen again.

In several other non-early-reader interviews, references were made to unsuccessful efforts to teach reading to preschool children for reasons other than a child's own interest. For instance, one mother recalled how she had spent "one whole Sunday" trying to teach her son the names of the letters. She explained, "I thought it was terrible that a child of four

didn't know the alphabet." Another mother of a non-early-reader described how she had once decided to teach her preschool daughter to
read by writing words on small cards. "But she learned nothing," the
mother added, "so that didn't last very long."

Another reason, perhaps, why preschool help "didn't last very long"
with some of the non-early-readers was the busy lives of their mothers.
In one home, for instance, the mother was "constantly occupied" with a
chronically ill parent. In another, the oldest child was "in and out of the
hospital since she was born," and this kept the mother "from doing anything extra" with the other two children. Another mother of a non-early-
reader said she was so busy that sometimes she did not have time to
answer the door or the telephone. However, impromptu questioning by
the interviewer identified no special reasons for her being so constantly
occupied and rushed. There were only two children in the family and,
according to the mother, her husband was "a very patient man" who
"spent a great deal of his free time with the boys."

In contrast to the portrayal of constantly occupied parents in some
of the non-early-reader families, not one mother of an early reader ever
used the word "busy" in talking about herself.[13] In general, these mothers
described the time they spent with their young children in a matter-of-
fact way. Several of the mothers, however, showed obvious enthusiasm
for the experiences they shared with the children. For instance, one
mother of an early reader talked about the many things she and her
young son had done together; and then she added, "Gee, I enjoyed that
child." Another mother of an early reader said she sometimes wondered
whether she herself was immature because she found the company of her
sons so much more stimulating than the time she spent with other adults.
Here she commented about the children's interesting questions and
observations which, she said, "made it sheer joy to be with them."

In some ways, the phrase "sheer joy" provides an appropriate introduction for a general conclusion that derives from the experience of interviewing the 60 New York parents and from studying the 60 reaction
reports. Perhaps this conclusion is "nothing more than common sense"
in its contention that early readers are not some unique species capable
of being identified and sorted by tests. Rather, it would seem, their preschool achievement in reading is the combined expression of themselves,
their parents, and the kinds of environment these parents provided. Such
a conclusion also suggests, of course, that the combination of factors
which led to preschool reading might also help to account for the fact
that, over the years, the early readers in this research continued to show
higher achievement in reading than the non-early-readers with whom
they were matched.

---

[13] In all 60 interviews, the word "busy" probably was used more often than any
other in the description of the subjects' fathers.

Chapter IX

Other Test Data in the Second Study

In the family interviews for this second study, some efforts were made to discover how the parents of the 30 early readers and the 30 non-early-readers viewed their children's personal traits and abilities. (The two groups were described very similarly by the parents.) This present chapter describes other efforts to identify the characteristics of these children. Three instruments were used: (1) a Teacher Rating Scale, (2) the Bender *Visual Motor Gestalt Test,* and (3) the *Minnesota Tests of Creative Thinking.*

The Teacher Rating Scale

In March of the first year of the New York study, each of these 60 children was rated by his teacher on traits and abilities which had been selected for one or both of the following reasons: (1) they were mentioned with relatively high frequency by parents in interviews; and (2) they were considered likely to be associated with preschool reading ability. The purpose of the ratings was to see how the early readers and the non-early-readers compared when they were observed in classroom situations, and by adults other than parents. The total list of characteristics and abilities for which ratings were requested can be found in Table 25. A copy of the Rating Scale itself comprises Appendix D.

Before the ratings are reported and discussed, some reminders about these data need to be made explicit. The first reminder could come from any parent, for it suggests that school behavior does not always match the behavior of children when they are at home. Speaking of her son, one research parent said, "When I talk about him with his teacher, it's as if she were talking about a child who isn't even mine."

That a rating might reflect the characteristics of the rater as much as the one being rated also makes it important to remember that many different teachers were describing the 60 subjects. At the start of the study, the children were enrolled in 23 different classrooms. By the end of the first year of the research—when teacher ratings were obtained—the children were in the same schools; however, one early reader had been double-promoted, and so he was in still another classroom. This meant that a total of 24 teachers were rating the 60 subjects.

A final point to keep in mind in connection with the teacher ratings is that the identification of the children who were the early readers was made known to teachers at the beginning of grade one. Whether this was forgotten because subsequent testings involved both early readers and non-early-readers is not known. Consequently it has to be assumed that the ratings of some teachers might have been affected by their knowledge of which children were the early readers. It must also be assumed that the assigned ratings for the various traits were not always independent. For example, a teacher's estimate of a child's memory might also affect his intelligence rating.

To minimize the effect of differences in intelligence among the 60 subjects, the teacher ratings were analyzed by comparing the two ratings on each trait for each of the 30 matched pairs of subjects. It will be recalled that the matching (each early reader with a non-early-reader) was done on the basis of Stanford–Binet IQ scores.

To illustrate, one question from the Teacher Rating Scale is presented here, followed by an account of how responses to it were analyzed.

How would you describe his memory? [1]
1. _____ Unusually poor
2. _____ Below average
3. _____ Average
4. _____ Above average
5. _____ Amazingly good

The two ratings given to each pair of subjects in response to this question about memory were compared. For instance, for one of the 30 pairs of subjects, a rating of "Amazingly good" was assigned to the early reader and a rating of "Above average" to the non-early-reader. These descriptions were recorded as a rating of 5 for the early reader and a rating of 4 for the non-early-reader. The difference score for the pair was noted as +1. With another pair of subjects the descriptions were reversed. The memory of the early reader was described as "Above average," which is given a numerical rating of 4, and the memory of the non-early-reader was described as "Amazingly good," given a rating of

---

[1] In the Teacher Rating Scale, a rating of 1 always indicated the minimum of whatever trait or ability was mentioned in a question. For example, in response to the question, "Is he self-reliant?" a rating of 1 indicated the child "Depends completely on others"; and a rating of 5 said he was "Extremely independent."

Table 25. Distribution of differences in teacher ratings, and mean differences, for 30 matched pairs of early readers and non-early-readers

Trait	4	3	2	1	0	−1	−2	−3	−4	$\overline{D}$
				Frequency of Difference Scores						
Intelligence	0	0	4	12	11	3	0	0	0	+0.6
Memory	0	0	4	13	11	2	0	0	0	+0.6
Persistence	0	0	0	12	14	3	1	0	0	+0.2
Competitiveness	0	0	3	11	10	5	1	0	0	+0.3
Work Habits [a] (Careless . . . Perfectionistic)	0	0	4	6	14	4	1	1	0	+0.2
Self-Reliance	0	0	5	8	14	3	0	0	0	+0.5
Attention to Job	0	2	4	12	4	3	4	1	0	+0.4
Tendency to Worry (Carefree . . . Anxious)	0	0	2	5	12	8	3	0	0	−0.2
Social Relationships (Submissive . . . Domineering)	0	1	0	7	19	2	1	0	0	+0.2
Attitude toward Adults (Indifferent . . . Eager to please)	0	0	0	12	17	1	0	0	0	+0.4
Curiosity	0	0	0	11	13	6	0	0	0	+0.2
Speaking Vocabulary	0	0	3	15	9	2	1	0	0	+0.6
Oral Communication	0	0	7	3	15	3	1	0	0	+0.4

[a] A description of the two extreme ratings is given when they might not be self-evident.

5. The two descriptions resulted in a difference score of −1 for this particular pair. In 11 instances, the rating assigned to an early reader was identical to the rating given the non-early-reader with whom he had been matched. For these 11 pairs, difference scores for memory were recorded as zero.

In the Teacher Rating Scale, thirteen traits and abilities were rated. Results of the ratings, recorded as difference scores, are summarized in Table 25.[2] Again, these data show close similarity between the early readers and non-early-readers as they were described by teachers. For example, none of the mean difference scores—shown in the last column in Table 25—is even as large as 1. In addition, individual difference scores of zero, indicating identical ratings for a pair of subjects, generally are the scores of highest frequency. In contrast, the largest possible difference score (4) was never found; even a difference score of 3 was rare. Thus, the data in Table 25 reinforce a finding that has pervaded this second study; namely, that except for achievement in reading and for certain family differences, the 30 early readers and the 30 non-early-readers appear to be very similar.

[2] The frequencies with which all available categories were used for the two groups of children can be found in Appendix D.

The Bender Visual Motor Gestalt Test

To collect additional information on the 30 early readers and the 30 non-early-readers, the *Visual Motor Gestalt Test* [3] was used in the second year of the research. This test was administered by research assistants in New York; but the data were analyzed by a psychologist in California who had made extensive use of the test in her work as a school psychologist.[4] A detailed description of this test can be found elsewhere [50]; here, a brief general description will be given.

The Bender *Gestalt Test* (as it is often called) is administered individually, and it has no time limits. Essentially it is a visual–motor test in which the task of the child being examined is to copy figures which appear on nine cards. The cards are shown, one at a time, by the test examiner. The child is equipped only with a pencil, eraser, and blank sheets of paper; no mechanical guides, such as a ruler, are permitted. While the child copies each figure, the examiner records observations about the child's test performance and about his behavior during the testing process.

For this research, the test examiners in New York used an observational outline designed to give a maximum amount of information to the psychologist in California who would be interpreting test results. The outline was developed, with the assistance of the psychologist, by following test prescriptions as they are described in the test manual. This outline gave detailed attention to (1) the child's approach to each of the nine tasks, (2) the child's procedures for reproducing each figure, and (3) the child's mannerisms and comments during the testing.

Prior to their use in this research, both the test and the observational outline were tried out with three children who were not subjects but who were seven years old. The practice testing was done in a one-way vision room allowing for observations of the testing and, later, for a discussion of testing and note-taking procedures.

For the research, the Bender *Gestalt* testing was done during the spring of the second year. Because of the special interest in the memory ability of the subjects, one step was added to the regular testing procedure. This step attempted to evaluate the child's memory, and was carried out in the following way.

When a subject finished reproducing the nine figures, the examiner talked about anything that seemed to be of interest to him. Approximately ten minutes later the examiner gave the child a blank sheet of paper and said: "I wonder whether you can remember what you saw on those nine cards I showed you. On this sheet of paper, draw as many figures as you can remember, and in any order. As you finish drawing

[3] By Loretta Bender. New York: American Orthopsychiatric Association, 1946.
[4] Here, this writer would like to express appreciation for the interest and the help of Miss Mary L. Brantly, assistant in research for the Oakland public schools.

Table 26. Distribution of differences in ratings based on Bender *Gestalt Test* data, and mean differences, for 30 matched pairs of early readers and non-early-readers

Trait	Frequency of Difference Scores							$\overline{D}$
	3	2	1	0	—1	—2	—3	
Intelligence	1	1	6	14	5	3	0	0.0
Memory	1	3	8	8	8	0	2	+0.1
Persistence	2	2	8	9	5	1	3	+0.1
Work habits [a] (Careless . . . Perfectionistic)	1	3	7	6	9	1	3	—0.1
Self-reliance	1	1	10	8	5	4	1	0.0
Attention to job	1	3	8	7	8	2	1	+0.1
Tendency to worry (Carefree . . . Anxious)	0	2	9	14	4	1	0	+0.2
Attitude toward adults (Indifferent . . . Eager to please)	0	2	9	9	10	0	0	+0.1

[a] A description of the two extreme ratings is given when they might not be self-evident.

each figure, I'll number it. Then, when you are finished, we can see how many you were able to remember. Take your time. There is no need to hurry."

When all of the testing was completed, the data were sent to the psychologist in California. For each of the 60 subjects, data were comprised of: (1) the drawings done while looking at the cards; (2) the drawings reproduced from memory, numbered in the order in which they were recalled; and (3) the test examiner's observational notes. Information about the sex and handedness of each subject also was supplied, but no identification of the early readers was made.

Using the various data, the psychologist rated each subject on eight traits. Selection of the traits was made on two bases: the traits had been included in the Teacher Rating Scale; and, secondly, the psychologist believed that the Bender *Gestalt* data could yield information about them.

With these Bender *Gestalt* data, ratings were made on 4-point rather than on 5-point scales.[5] The 4-point scale was selected because it would not permit the use of "average" ratings as an easy and convenient way to settle uncertainties. Without "average" ratings, it was reasoned, possible differences between the early readers and the non-early-readers might be made more apparent.

What became apparent is summarized in Table 26. This table lists the eight traits, and shows the distribution of differences in the ratings

[5] It will be recalled that the teacher ratings were made on 5-point scales.

assigned to each pair of subjects (early reader and non-early-reader). The calculation of these differences followed the procedure used with the data from the Teacher Rating Scale. However, since a 4-point scale was used with the Bender *Gestalt* data, the greatest possible difference in ratings for each pair of subjects was 3 rather than 4.[6]

A quick but accurate response to the data presented in Table 26 is to say that, again, they indicate the 30 early readers and the 30 non-early-readers were very similar—at least in their performance on the Bender *Gestalt Test*, and in their behavior during the testing process.[7]

Tests of Creative Thinking

One other attempt was made in the New York study to identify possible differences between the 30 early readers and the 30 non-early-readers who were comparably bright in relation to Stanford–Binet IQ's. This attempt involved use of Torrance's *Minnesota Tests of Creative Thinking* in the spring of the third year of the research [96].

In 1958, when the California study began, widespread interest in "creativity" was just developing. The title of an article appearing in *Phi Delta Kappan* that same year gives a capsule picture of the new interest: "The Meaning of 'Giftedness'—An Examination of an Expanding Concept" [39]. Subsequently, expansion of the concept of giftedness occurred quickly, and in the direction of creativity.

Probably because the earliest reports of the California study were published at a time when creativity was a very popular topic, readers of the reports often raised questions about the relationship between early reading and the factor of creativity. Basic to almost all the questioning were two assumptions: (1) Reading achievement, especially in its initial stages, demands a kind of rigidity rather than creativity. (2) Early readers are probably rigid rather than creative kinds of children. The questions provoked this writer's curiosity. Their frequency prompted use of the *Minnesota Tests of Creative Thinking* in the New York study. A brief description of these tests follows.

The Abbreviated Form VII was used for the research; it consists of four subtests. Ten minutes are allowed for each. The tests were administered individually and orally to insure that responses to the two verbal subtests would not be inhibited by the subjects' inability to write what they wanted to say. Instead, the test examiner did the writing for them. The test Manual suggests this procedure when the children being tested are not yet in fourth grade.

Subtests 1 and 2 are labeled "nonverbal." Subtest 1 requires the

[6] The frequencies with which available ratings were used to describe early readers and non-early-readers are shown in Appendix E.

[7] Very often the Bender *Gestalt Test* is used to identify possible organic difficulties. No such difficulties were apparent in any of the test results for the 60 subjects.

completion of ten figures. The directions to the pupil (read from the Manual) describe the task:

> By adding lines to the figures . . . you can sketch some interesting objects or pictures. Try to think of some picture or object that no one else will think of. Try to make it tell as complete and as interesting a story as you can by adding to and building up your first idea. Make up a title for each of your drawings. [96:3]

Subtest 2 is similar except that the child makes objects or pictures by adding lines to circles.

Subtest 3, called "Product Improvement," is a verbal test. It, too, can be described by quoting directions from the Manual:

> At the bottom of this page is a sketch of a stuffed toy dog. . . . In the spaces on this page and on the next one, list the cleverest, most interesting and unusual ways you can think of for changing this toy dog so that children will have more fun playing with it. [96:4]

Subtest 4, headed "Unusual Uses of Tin Cans," is also verbal. Once more, the Manual can be quoted to indicate the nature of the test:

> Most people throw their empty cans away, but they have thousands of interesting and unusual uses. In the spaces below and on the next page, list as many interesting and unusual uses as you can think of. . . . Do not limit yourself to uses you have seen or heard about; think about as many possible new uses as you can. [96:5]

The research assistants who were administering reading tests also administered the *Minnesota Tests of Creative Thinking*. However, this writer scored all of them. To avoid any bias in the scoring, tests were identified by number rather than by the names of subjects. What became quickly apparent, though, was that it was easier to conceal a subject's name than it was to evaluate his test performance.

In scoring the tests, every effort was made to follow very closely the directions in the Manual. In addition, to achieve maximum consistency in the evaluations, each subtest for the 60 subjects was scored over a period of two days or less. In spite of the care and precautions, however, there can be no guarantee that the scoring was absolutely accurate, because the nature of the tests requires some very arbitrary decisions in each evaluation. Moreover, in the opinion of this writer—and the same reaction has been stated by at least one other researcher—there is no way to judge whether subjects who received the highest scores were, in fact, the most creative children [40]. Actually, the scoring process constantly raised questions about whether the tests measured true creativity or mere nonconformity. The tests also prompted a question about the possibility of measuring creativity with tasks that are timed.

In spite of the many unsettling questions, the tests were scored; and results are summarized in Table 27. Each child was scored on four variables: fluency, flexibility, originality, and elaboration. Procedures for assigning numerical values for each variable are described in the test manual [96].

Table 27. Achievement of 30 early readers and 30 non-early-readers on the Minnesota Tests of Creative Thinking

| Subtests | Mean Score | | Difference between Means | Standard Error of Difference |
	EARLY READERS	NON-EARLY- READERS		
Verbal				
Fluency	25.2	27.4	2.2	15.4
Flexibility	13.5	14.5	1.0	6.8
Originality	10.8	12.3	1.5	8.4
Elaboration	3.8	4.1	0.3	5.8
Nonverbal				
Fluency	21.4	22.4	1.0	7.6
Flexibility	15.9	16.8	0.9	6.0
Originality	15.1	15.0	0.1	8.0
Elaboration	64.1	65.7	1.6	27.5

For both the verbal and the nonverbal tests, a comparison of the two mean scores for each variable indicates that differences between those of the early readers and those of the non-early-readers were very small. On the verbal subtests, differences ranged from 0.3 to 2.2; on the nonverbal subtests, from 0.1 to 1.6. Thus the largest difference for any variable on either verbal or nonverbal tests was 2.2. However, even for this difference no statistical evaluation of the null hypothesis is required. As the data in Table 27 indicate, the size of each difference, in relation to its standard error, is less than 1. Consequently it must be concluded that the average achievement of the early readers was not significantly different from that of the non-early-readers in relation to the variables of fluency, flexibility, originality, and elaboration, as measured in these tests. To put these data into a larger context: findings from creative thinking tests, as well as those from the Teacher Rating Scale and the Bender *Gestalt Test,* indicate that a group of early readers and a group of non-early-readers were very similar.

Chapter X

New York Case Studies

Selection of children for the New York case studies was accompanied by the temptation to choose children whose ways of life could only be found in a city as big and diversified as New York. The child whose mother lived the life of a beatnik in Greenwich Village, the child whose father was "so busy making money" that his son never missed him when the father suddenly died of a heart attack—such children certainly would be "interesting" subjects for case studies. But because this is a research report and not potential material for a best-seller list, selection followed the procedures used in the first study. The one difference is that non-early-readers, as well as early readers, are included.

First, early readers were chosen from the group of 30 whose families were interviewed. As in the California research, the early readers selected are those who had the lowest and the highest Stanford–Binet IQ's and the lowest and highest reading scores at the start of first grade.

Following each case study of an early reader, a case study of the non-early-reader with whom the early reader had been paired for the research will be given.

The presentation of each case study begins with information about the child's race and sex, socioeconomic status, chronological age at the start of first grade, and Stanford–Binet IQ. For each early reader information is given about his reading achievement at the beginning of first grade and at the end of the research (after three years of school). For non-early-readers, the terminal reading-achievement level will be noted.

In all case studies, fictitious names are used.

Early Reader: JACK
Lowest IQ
                                    Caucasian boy; LM socioeconomic status;
                            CA=5.9; IQ=99; initial reading grade=2.5;
                                        terminal reading grade=5.1.

"Very competitive," "must win," "tries to compete with his brother in everything," "always wants to be the best," "has got to top everyone" —these were the kinds of descriptions of Jack that predominated in the interview with his mother. Jack's brother, frequently referred to as the source of his competitive spirit, was the older of the two children in the family. When Jack was starting first grade, his brother was entering fifth.

Both parents were natives of New York City. They were high school graduates, but neither had attended college. At the time of the interview the father worked as an office manager. He was described as having little time to spend with the children because of long hours at the office, and because the family lived far from his place of employment. According to the mother, her husband's greatest influence on their sons was in the area of sports. The mother said their younger son easily memorized all kinds of minute details about sportsmen (batting averages, birth places, uniform numbers), and that he and his father "were full of sports talk" whenever they spent time together. As viewed by the mother, Jack's father played no part in the child's early achievement in reading. It was her opinion that an interest in "constant scribbling," combined with a good memory and an eagerness to copy everything his older brother did, were the reasons why Jack began to read, even before kindergarten.

In the course of this interview, Jack also was described by the mother as "terribly active"—as a child who "always has to be doing two or three things at a time." It was at this point in the interview that the mother mentioned how Jack was "always, always writing," even while he watched favorite television programs. The mother also recalled that it was the weather reports on television which initially stimulated her younger son's interest in learning to print. Prior to kindergarten, she explained, Jack watched a television nursery school program almost every morning; yet it was the weather reports and, later, the television commercials that seemed to create his excitement about letters, spelling, writing, and then reading. She said she herself was unaware of Jack's ability to identify written words until he began reading aloud some of the advertisements on television. She said his recognition of the same words on food products in the grocery store was "a source of great delight for him." At the time, she said, Jack was about four.

Meanwhile, Jack's older brother was in school, and the mother was helping with his homework. About this the mother commented, "Jack never missed a session." As a result, she said, he "began to pick up sounds of letters," and to ask for help with printing. According to the mother, most of the help came from the brother. She said she herself always answered Jack's questions, but she felt uneasy about doing more because she "didn't know how to teach." The mother also mentioned feeling no special need to help her preschool son with reading because she had read "some place" that children who read early "do not stay ahead of the others."

In response to interview questions about Jack's years in kindergarten and first grade, the mother said she was especially pleased with the kindergarten experience because "Jack learned he couldn't always be the winner." In describing first grade, she said he "only became excited when there was something new to learn." The mother also mentioned that her younger son was "not too excited about first grade" because he had read "all of the first-grade books" when he was five. At that time a "favorite cousin" was in first grade, and the children read together.

The mother also mentioned, in the course of the interview, that the great current interest of Jack was to learn how to do cursive writing "because that's what the big boys do."

Non-Early-Reader
Paired with Jack: LUCY   Caucasian girl; UM socioeconomic status;
                                     CA=6.6; IQ=104; terminal reading grade=6.4.

The non-early-reader with whom Jack had been paired was Lucy. Like Jack, Lucy was from a Jewish family. Unlike Jack, however, her parents were college graduates. The father was a lawyer, "just getting started." The mother had prepared to be a teacher, but she married following graduation from college. One year later, Lucy was born. When Lucy was two, a brother was born. At the time of the research interview, Lucy was six and her brother was four. This younger child was present for all of the interview; it is possible that his presence helped to explain why the mother talked about him as much as about her daughter, even though the daughter was central to most of the research questions.

In general, the mother's responses to all of the questions were brief, and sometimes even abrupt. When she seemed unable to answer a question about Lucy, she would often say something like, "Oh, she's always been such a busy little girl, I never paid too much attention." From the mother's comments, though, it appeared that she gave much time and attention to Lucy's brother.

In describing her children, the mother depicted Lucy as a child who was "full of energy" with a "bubbly personality." When alone, the mother explained, Lucy was content with quiet activities and especially liked "any kind of art work." "She was always making something," the mother commented as she recollected earlier years. When playing with other children, however, Lucy "did nothing but run." Asked for a more specific description of her daughter's play activities, the mother said, "I really don't know. She's always had lots of friends, and they just played."

It was at this point in the interview that Lucy was contrasted with her brother. The mother said her son did not like to play with other

children, and so she herself "kept him amused." She described the boy as a child who was "placid," "calm and quiet," and "unable to play alone." "He always wants to be with me," she said. The son this mother described with obvious fondness was a very handsome child. He appeared to be quiet but alert, and also more interested than his mother in the research interview.

As the interview progressed, it was learned that Lucy showed some preschool interest in identifying written words, but the mother was unable to recall with certainty at what age the interest initially developed. The mother said she read to the two children "just about every day," and that probably it was this reading that led to Lucy's curiosity about words. However, the mother also said she felt parents should not try to teach preschool children to read, or "to do arithmetic," because "it might mix them up." She said home instruction would "interfere with the teacher's methods."

Often, during the interview, the mother referred to Lucy's high and quick achievement in first grade, particularly in reading. Several times she described her daughter as "the best reader in her room." The mother said Lucy was then reading "about an hour every night," and that she no longer wanted to be read to.

The only time Lucy's father was mentioned in the interview was when direct questions about him were asked. It appeared that he worked long and irregular hours, that he spent little time with the children, and that when he was at home he did "a lot of legal reading connected with his work."

Early Reader: JEAN
Highest IQ and Highest Initial
Reading Achievement   Caucasian girl; UM socioeconomic status;
                                    CA=6.3; IQ=170; initial reading grade=5.2;
                                    terminal reading grade=10.7

Of the 156 early readers in the New York study, Jean had the highest IQ and also the highest reading score at the start of first grade. At the time this writer interviewed her mother (October), the *Stanford–Binet Intelligence Scale* had not been given to Jean. However, all the interview data indicated very high intelligence. Her IQ of 170, therefore, did not come as a surprise.

Jean was the older of the two children in the family. At the time Jean was ready for first grade, her brother was four. The children's parents were European-born, but the mother spoke with no sign of a foreign accent. She explained that both she and her husband "came to this country at an early age."

Jean's mother and father married while the mother was in college, but she remained in school long enough to graduate. The father was a physician, and "very busy." However, several times during the interview the mother mentioned that he spent as much time as possible with the children, and that Jean "especially liked to take walks with her father." The family owned a home in a middle-class neighborhood in New York City.

According to interview data, Jean's behavior indicated high intelligence "practically from birth." Her mother commented, "She walked early (10 months), and has always been like a little adult." The mother also referred to Jean's early interest in books, and to the way she had enjoyed being read to "ever since she was about a year old." The mother mentioned that both she and her husband were "avid readers," and that both enjoyed reading to the children. She said her husband especially liked poetry, and that when he read to Jean it was generally from a book of rhymes. The mother believed it was this kind of reading that led to Jean's preschool interest in the sounds of words, and then in the sounds of particular letters.

Earlier, however, Jean had learned the names of the letters. "She was about three then," the mother recalled. The mother also recalled how she used to buy "little books for the children in the supermarket," among them several picture dictionaries. The mother felt it was these books in particular that excited Jean's curiosity about the names of letters. This interest, the mother explained, was followed by attempts to write the letters. The mother said she gave Jean help with printing "whenever she asked for it."

When the mother was questioned about the age at which her daughter began to print and to read, she said she was uncertain whether the reading or the writing came first, and for the following reason. At about three, Jean was copying letters, and then words, from the simple picture books that had been read to her. At the same time, however, she was also at least pretending to read the books. The mother said she herself assumed Jean had memorized the stories, and so paid "little attention." However, when Jean was about four, the mother recalled, "I began to wonder whether she was memorizing or really reading, and so I printed some of the words on little cards." As it turned out, Jean identified all of them. "That's the first time I really knew she could read," the mother said. And then she added, "From that time on, I paid more attention to her questions about words."

By itself, this parental account of the way a precocious daughter learned to read early does not give a complete picture of Jean. For, in the interview, the mother also provided information about social aspects of the child's development. According to the mother, Jean's "ease in learning" was coupled with "a lack of ease in social relationships," especially with children. She played with other children, the mother said, but "probably because she knew we expected her to." "They're too silly," Jean was apt to say, or "They're too rough." The mother did say, though, that Jean really enjoyed the company of other children "when she could get them to play imaginative games," or "when they'd play school and let her be the teacher." Here the mother also recalled that Jean enjoyed

124 CHILDREN WHO READ EARLY

"making up plays based on stories that had been read to her," and that she was willing to play with her younger brother "when he was willing to assume a subordinate role in one of her plays."

This discussion about Jean's lack of interest in children her own age led to comments about Jean's year in kindergarten. The mother said she herself was very grateful to the kindergarten teacher "because she showed such interest in individual children, and really helped Jean." Jean's own response to kindergarten, the mother said, began with fear, changed to interest, and ended in boredom. The mother also believed that Jean was bored with first grade, and quoted the child's most frequent comment about it: "I already know what the teacher keeps telling us."

Non-Early-Reader
Paired with Jean: ANDY   Caucasian boy; UL socioeconomic status;
                                  CA=6.6; IQ=161; terminal reading grade=7.4.

Of all the words that were spoken by Andy's mother during the research interview, it seemed the word "play" was used most frequently. Almost every description of Andy referred to his great interest in active, outdoor play. "He can go from morning 'til night," the mother said at one point. Another time she commented, "Andy always has a ball in his hands." And at still another point in the interview the mother observed, "He doesn't like to just sit. He's a very active boy, always playing with something."

This mother appeared to be very accepting of her son and quietly proud. In assessing his accomplishments she especially emphasized his quick achievement in reading, in first grade. She also mentioned that the ease with which he was learning to read surprised her because he showed so little interest in books at home.

This particular observation about Andy prompted the mother to contrast him with a sister who was six years older, and "in an IGC class" (class for intellectually gifted children). The mother's description of the daughter during her preschool years included the comment, "She always walked around the house with a pad and pencil." Later the mother added, "She was even reading before she went to school." The opinion of the mother was that these children were both "very bright," but "just different types." The daughter "always had her head in a book," while Andy "never stopped running." Here the mother mentioned that she would have been glad to help Andy with reading before he started school—"the way I helped my daughter"—but that he had never shown much interest. And then the mother commented, "I don't like to force them. I don't want to give them a dislike for something before they start."

There was a third child in the family, a boy who was four years younger than Andy. Little was said about him. At the time of the interview this youngest child was napping.

Andy's family occupied what appeared to be a very small apartment in a city housing project. The living room, in which the interview was held, was clean and neat but modestly furnished.

When asked about her husband's occupation, Andy's mother said he worked in a bank. A question about the nature of the work only brought forth, "He does a variety of things." According to the mother, Andy's father had graduated from high school, but she herself had not. Prior to her marriage she had worked as a machine operator in a factory. Both parents were natives of New York City. All of the children's grandparents had been born in Italy.

From what could be learned in a single interview, this family appeared to be a happy, close-knit group. The comments of the mother indicated that she and her husband were very proud of their children, recognized their abilities, but also were aware of the differences among the children. It appeared, too, that the family spent much time together, doing "whatever the kids wanted to do."

Early Reader: MARK
Lowest Initial Reading Achievement

Caucasian boy; UM socioeconomic status;
CA=6.3; IQ=115; initial reading grade=1.5;
terminal reading grade=4.8.

One of the 156 early readers in the New York study entered first grade with a reading grade-level score of 1.4. However, this child was not in the special experimental group and so his family had not been interviewed. Of the eight early readers who had initial scores of 1.5, two were in the special experimental group. One of these, Mark, was randomly selected for the case studies.

Mark's family lived in a large, ostentatiously furnished apartment in one of the wealthier sections of New York City. Occupants of the apartment were the father and mother, two sons, and a maid.

Mark's father was European-born, but came to the United States at an early age. He completed his high school education by going to night school. At the time of the research interview he owned his own business, which kept him so busy that the family generally saw him only on Sundays; at certain times of the year, he even worked a seven-day week. The mother mentioned that the younger of their sons, Mark, "saw so little of his father" that he was very shy with him. She mentioned, too, that Mark called his father by his first name, and that he had to be encouraged "to go to him," when the father was home. She said her husband was "hurt by this," but felt unable to spend more time with the family.

Like that of her husband, the formal education of Mark's mother ended with high school graduation. Before her marriage, she worked in a department store. In the family's "TV room," where the research interview was carried on, the mother called attention to a large collection of framed photographs of herself and her husband posed with "famous night club entertainers." The pictures were autographed, and covered about half of two walls. They gave the interviewer the impression that Mark's father was considerably older than his mother.

Mark was the younger of two sons. He was six, at the time of the interview, and his brother was nine. The mother often spoke of the slowness of her older son, and of how she had had to help with his homework from the time he started school. She said this help went on "every single night." She also said that Mark had always been eager "to get into the middle of it," but that she discouraged his participation for two reasons. First, she said, it was so difficult to teach the older boy that she needed to give all of her attention to it. In addition, she wanted to avoid emphasizing the slowness of her older son by having "a younger one around who picks up everything with one explanation."

To discourage Mark's participation in the homework sessions, the mother encouraged him to watch television instead. She also purchased "a bundle of books" to keep him occupied. Upon examination, many of these books turned out to be children's "teach yourself" workbooks of a kind often found in drug and department stores. Most were concerned with arithmetic, but one provided help with phonics and another showed a child how to print. The mother maintained, though, that it was the television programs, and especially the commercials, that really sparked her younger son's early curiosity about numbers, and then about words. She recalled Mark's interest in the numbers on the television dial, and how this led to many comments and questions about numbers appearing on such things as clocks and street signs. It was at this point that the mother mentioned that Mark's early ability to tell time ("He was the only child starting kindergarten who could tell time") was the result of his special interest in numbers. In fact, in the course of the interview it was very apparent that Mark's mother was much more aware of his "number ability" than of his early reading. She said, "He has a mind for numbers just like his father's." She also commented that Mark's most frequent request was "Make me some problems."

Asked whether she had given Mark any early help with reading, the mother said, "I tried to answer his questions." At a later point in the interview she said, "We sometimes talked about the sounds of letters. I was hoping he'd learn to figure out the words himself." Here, the mother again remarked about the amount of time she had to give to the older son, and about the fatigue and tension she felt as a result.

Although Mark's mother frequently spoke about the slowness of her older son, she made very few comments about his personality. In contrast, she spoke freely and frequently about Mark's temperament. Most often Mark was described by such expressions as "defiant," "insists on doing things his way," "must have the last word," "wants to be correct all the time." When the mother was asked, "If someone else were to take care of Mark, what would you feel was important for her to know about him?" she quickly responded, "I'd tell her to be firm with him."

Later, when she was asked whether she had any special ambitions or hopes for Mark, the mother said, "His father wants him to be a doctor." [1] And then she added, "Money will be no problem."

Non-Early-Reader
Paired with Mark: STEVE   Caucasian boy; LU socioeconomic status; CA=6.1; IQ=108; terminal reading grade=5.2.

The non-early-reader paired with Mark was Steve. The mother of Steve was a very articulate person who responded to interview questions with vivid descriptions and a wealth of details. In addition, she was quick to inform this writer that the interview had been granted only "to let Columbia people know about the need for a junior high school in the community." With this kind of motive in the background, the interview proceeded in a surprisingly pleasant manner.

In this family, the father was part-owner of a business which had been started by his father-in-law. The spacious and luxurious apartment occupied by the family suggested that the business was extremely successful.

Although Steve's father was a college graduate, the mother had completed only two years in a junior college. At the time of the interview the couple had three children, all boys. Steve was the oldest. The next boy was a year younger, and the other brother was four years younger. It was while describing these children that the mother remarked, "I have not let Steve depend upon me for help with his school work because I couldn't possibly help three of them."

To help with the children, however, there was a full-time maid. On the day of the interview a second woman was in the apartment, ironing. The mother explained that she came "a couple times a week" to help with the laundry and ironing.

Answers to many of the interview questions about Steve began with the comment, "He is just like his mother." Asked for some elaboration, the mother did not hesitate to point out that he was "high-strung," "a decided perfectionist," and "a worrier." At one point the mother also added, "He memorizes easily."

This "tendency to memorize" was referred to again when the mother told how she used to read to Steve, but stopped when he was about four. At that age, she explained, "He started memorizing all the stories." Asked why she was concerned about the memorization, the mother stated very emphatically that she "didn't want him to memorize words." "I want them sounded out," she said.

At about the time Steve's mother had stopped reading to him, she was enrolling him in a private nursery school. Her descriptions of the school were always negative: "Those nursery schools employ young

---

[1] This question was asked out of curiosity, not because it was one of the standard interview questions.

girls rather than mature women," she said once; and again, "I think the teachers are people who can't get a job in a kindergarten or in the elementary schools."

In contrast, the mother's reaction to Steve's year in a public school kindergarten was extremely positive. She felt the kindergarten had been very successful in teaching him "to get along with thirty other children." She also felt her son's kindergarten teacher was "a tremendous person." Here the mother recalled how this teacher had warned her not to help Steve with reading because it would cause problems for him later on. The mother said that his "tremendous reading progress" in first grade convinced her of the correctness of the kindergarten teacher's advice.

In discussing the years prior to Steve's entrance into first grade, the mother was asked whether he had ever shown any interest in learning to print or write. She said, "Oh yes, but that was soon discouraged." Asked why she had curbed this particular interest, the mother commented, "He used to mess up the house, and once even wrote on the wall." After that, she explained, "I purchased coloring books for him, but he was allowed to use them only under supervision."

At the time this interview took place, Steve's main interest, according to his mother, was television. "He watches whatever he wants to watch," she said, and added, "It makes him lazy, but it keeps him quiet."

These brief case studies conclude the description of the second study of preschool reading. Prior to a final discussion of the two studies, in the last chapter, the next chapter will present observations on some educational and psychological ideas that were prominent in 1964, the year the second study ended.

Chapter **XI**

After 1961: Developing
Concerns and Trends

In Chapter VI, attention was given to certain changes that were occurring between September, 1958, when the first study of early readers began, and September, 1961, the beginning of the second study. Two trends especially pertinent to the studies were strongly established by 1961. One was engulfing the schools with the insistence that more "content" ought to be taught, and at earlier ages. The other was a growing interest in the unique importance of the young child's environment and the learning opportunities it provided. There was also, however, a contrary mood persisting in some quarters: "Why hurry?"

That was 1961, very briefly described. Now it is appropriate to ask about the year in which the studies came to an end. Was 1964 characterized by similar concerns? A quick but accurate answer is: Yes, only more so. However, to provide a slightly more detailed framework for the concluding discussion of the research, this chapter will present a brief account of some key developments between 1961 and 1964 in the more important trends related to young children's education.

The Trend toward Earlier Reading

In November of 1961, two months after the start of the second study, an article entitled "Questions That Need Asking" appeared in the *Teachers College Record*. Its author was the well-known anthropologist Margaret Mead. Some of the interestingly provocative "questions that need asking" were very directly related to the concerns of this writer's research. For example:

. . . what is the real basis of our present belief that children should be taught how to read *in school*? Originally, reading was taught as an apprenticeship skill by one who could read to one who wanted to learn. It was only when societies wished to change the proportions of literacy within a generation that schools were needed in which the children of non-literate parents could be taught in bunches. But today America's is an almost completely literate society. Why shouldn't mothers, who spend all day with their children, teach them to read, to understand money, to think about numbers, to understand the calendar, the clock, time, space? Now that these are the necessary requirements for a full humanity, just as walking and talking and understanding kinship relations and the local terrain were once the requirements for a full humanity, why can't all such essentials be taught at home? Do we know why not? [70:92]

What Mead introduced as rhetorical questioning received a variety of answers between 1961 and 1964. One rather unsettling type went directly from publishers to parents *via* newspaper advertisements and popular magazine articles. The promotional character of such "answers" is revealed in a widely discussed *Ladies Home Journal* article that appeared in May, 1963. The article, "You Can Teach Your Baby to Read," claimed:

The best time to teach your child to read with little or no trouble is when he is about two years old. Beyond two years of age, the teaching of reading gets harder every year. . . . If you are willing to go to a little trouble, you can begin when your baby is 18 months old or—if you are very clever—as early as 10 months. [26:62]

At the conclusion of the article, an advertisement for a teaching kit for parents appeared. Subsequently, similar advertisements could be found in newspapers throughout the country.

Certain other magazines, some with fairly wide circulation, presented articles with more temperate themes—and without pressures on parents to invest in teaching materials. In fact, many dealt with the responsibility of the school for earlier reading. During 1963, three relevant articles appeared in *Saturday Review* [45, 57, 101]. The first, in July, was written by a school curriculum coordinator who emphasized that "kindergarten no longer needs to serve as a major socializing agency" [57]. The author also stressed the need for schools to make more appropriate provisions for the intellectual differences found among five-year-olds.

The other two 1963 *Saturday Review* articles appeared in November. The theme of one paralleled the point of view expressed in the July issue. This article was written by a kindergarten teacher who made a plea for kindergarten programs that challenge the "sophisticated, TV indoctrinated five-year-old." At the same time, the author questioned the appropriateness of attempts to find easy solutions in workbook-oriented programs [45].

The other article, by a nursery school teacher, presented a contrary point of view. Asking, "Is Play Obsolete?" it was critical of "the hurrier" —one who "either out of forgetfulness or of dislike of his own childhood . . . tries to rob today's children of theirs" [101].

During the 1961–1964 period, some articles in professional journals also voiced opposition to "the hurrier." Most were found in *Childhood Education* [17, 51, 52]. Later, some of the *Childhood Education* articles were reprinted in a bulletin prepared by the Association for Childhood Education International and called *Reading in the Kindergarten?* [84]

Little research about pre-first-grade reading was reported during these years. Some articles that did appear were observational accounts of reading in the kindergarten, often written by kindergarten teachers [4, 69, 91, 97]. The research of O. K. Moore with computerized typewriters was still going on; but reports of his findings could be found only in nonprofessional magazines. One of these, written by Maya Pines, appeared in a 1963 issue of *Harper's* [79]: "How Three-Year-Olds Teach Themselves to Read—and Love It."

Trends in Other Areas

A portrayal which focuses on opinions about earlier reading is merely a partial view of the times. Other concerns of this 1961–1964 period must be mentioned, if only to show that the interest in earlier reading was but one dimension of a many-sided theme. Essentially, the broader theme echoed with optimistic viewpoints both about the intellectual potential of young children and about the advantages of, and even the need for, earlier schooling.

During these years, the question of earlier entrance into school gained widespread attention through a new interest in an old problem: Children from the lowest of socioeconomic levels start school with disadvantages that preclude adequate achievement. One of the earliest manifestations of concerted interest in the problem was a conference on "Pre-School Enrichment of Socially Disadvantaged Children," held in December of 1962, "to explore . . . the possibilities of accelerating the cognitive development of young children, beyond what might be expected from a standard nursery school situation" [24].

Later, in 1963, a conference on "Education in Depressed Areas" was held at Teachers College, Columbia University. Published proceedings of the conference included a paper by Martin Deutsch, a psychologist who came to be closely associated with the education of children commonly categorized as "socially disadvantaged" or "culturally deprived." In his paper, Deutsch described researches under his direction at the Institute for Developmental Studies, part of the New York Medical College. The assumption being tested by many of the studies was that "early intervention by well-structured programs will significantly reduce the attenuating influence of the socially marginal environment" [23]. Later, in a 1964 issue of *Life,* the work of Deutsch and his associates received national attention [10]. By 1964, however, there still was no accumulation of research findings sufficient to provide detailed guidelines for appropriate and productive school programs. The lack of serviceable data, however, had little effect on the move toward pre-kindergarten classes for culturally deprived children. The need was apparent, the children were available, and the classes began.

Meanwhile, other researchers in other classrooms were working with the possibility that earlier schooling might have some advantages for the mentally retarded. In 1958, an investigation reported by Samuel A. Kirk had been optimistic in its findings [59]. During the 1961–1964 period, another major study also appeared. Called "The Effects of a Preschool Program upon Young Educable Retarded Children," this was a report of a mental retardation project carried on between 1957 and 1961, and published in 1962 [30]. The research had many ancillary objectives, but its essential purpose was to develop and to evaluate an experimental curriculum for young retardates. One criterion for admission into the preschool groups was a chronological age of no less than 4 years 9 months and of no more than 6 years 9 months. Another was an IQ between 50 and 75. Among the positive effects of the experimental program were IQ increments and, subsequent to the program itself, achievement scores in reading that were higher than would be anticipated.

Still another trend relating to pre-first-grade children must be mentioned in this quick survey. This was the continuation of interest in Montessori education. Revived in the 1950's, the interest was even greater in the 1960's. In fact, Montessori classes for children younger than six sprang up throughout the country. In these classes the Montessori materials were present, but classroom observers did not always witness teachers who reflected sufficient Montessori training. One result was surprising variety in the implementation of Montessori theory.

Meanwhile, The American Montessori Society was founded, and in 1962 its first president wrote *Learning How to Learn* [83]. The theme was the adaptation of Montessori philosophy to American education, and the book included a lengthy bibliography of materials about Maria Montessori and her work. Later, there was the promise of new editions of older books written by and about Montessori. One of the first, *The Montessori Method*, appeared in 1964 [72].

And so the 1960's moved on—headed very much in the direction of earlier schooling for more children, but with a minimum of facts to guide the way. It is within such a context that this writer's two studies of early readers ended, and it is within the same framework that a discussion of findings is presented. If the reader senses caution in the discussion, it is because caution was intended.

Chapter **XII**

Summary and Implications of the Findings

The findings of the research have been reported and discussed in previous chapters. This final chapter will highlight only those data which would be of special interest to professional educators and to parents of young children. At the start, the chapter summarizes answers to questions that guided the development of the research. Later, comments will be made about some of the implications of the findings for early childhood education and for school efforts to teach beginning reading.

What Is the Effect of an Earlier Start on Later Achievement in Reading?

In the context of this report, an "earlier start" means reading that began at home, prior to first grade. Children reported to have received help with reading in kindergarten were excluded as possible subjects. While this decision probably eliminated some children who did begin to read at home, the concern of the research was early reading achievement that resulted only from help or instruction not given in school.

When the initial study began in 1958, it was rather generally assumed that early readers would have problems later. The predictions took a variety of forms, most often one of the following: beginning too soon, early readers would be bored later; or, learning from someone not trained to teach, they would later be confused.

The findings in these two studies in no way corroborate the pessimistic predictions about the future achievement of early readers. Even after six years of school instruction in reading, the early readers, as a group, maintained their lead in achievement over classmates of the same mental age who did not begin to read until the first grade.

133

Admittedly, the number of early readers in each of the two studies was small. In addition, both groups of subjects were subdivided for some comparisons into still smaller groups (boys and girls, double-promoted and non-double-promoted children). Consequently it would be bold or naïve, or both, to suggest that this research provides final answers to the questions it posed about the effect of an earlier start on future achievement in reading. As a minimum, however, the findings do suggest the need for an informed and systematic reevaluation of some older notions about a start in reading that begins before the first grade.

It is possible, too, that the especially high achievement of the bright students who were double-promoted is evidence of the productivity of school instruction that recognizes and accommodates individual differences. Such accommodation hardly existed in those first-grade classrooms in which early readers seem to have been treated as if they had not yet begun to read. More flexible reading programs in first grade could have offered more appropriate challenge to the early readers, without risking the adjustment problems which sometimes accompany double promotion.

What Kinds of Children Tend to Be Early Readers?

It would be natural to assume that precociousness in reading is one manifestation of intellectual superiority. And indeed the median IQ's of the two groups of early readers in this research were high (121 in California and 133 in New York). However, within the groups, the IQ scores showed great variation. The significance of the wide ranges of IQ scores (91 to 161 in California, 82 to 170 in New York) must not be overlooked. Nor must the research data—especially in the first study—which suggested that the value of an early start might be especially great for children with the lower IQ's. It was hypothesized in Chapter III that the less bright children might have profited from their preschool start in reading because it provided additional time to achieve. In turn, the extra years would allow for a slower learning pace and for extra practice, two factors that could be of particular importance for children not blessed with especially high IQ's.

These foregoing comments assume, of course, that the Stanford–Binet IQ's achieved by the early readers in the first year of the research accurately described their intelligence. There are those who would question the validity of an intelligence test administered at the age of six or seven. However, the work of Benjamin S. Bloom, summarized in a 1964 publication called *Stability and Change in Human Characteristics*, moves toward more optimistic conclusions [11]. Bloom writes:

> . . . we may conclude that the correlation between intelligence [when ideally measured] at age 3 and age 17 is about +.65, between intelligence measured at age 5 and age 17 is about +.80, and between intelligence measured at age 8 and age 17 is almost +.90. [11:61]

Variables other than intelligence were also of concern in the research, especially because of findings in the first study. In that initial phase of the research only early readers were studied in detail, and findings suggested that certain personality characteristics might be associated with preschool reading.' However, the comparison of early readers and comparably bright non-early-readers in the second study was remarkably consistent in pointing to similarities rather than to differences between the groups. Data collected in home interviews and, later, by means of a teacher rating scale, the Bender *Gestalt Test,* and the *Minnesota Tests of Creative Thinking* showed the early readers and the non-early-readers to be very similar in relation to the traits and characteristics selected for study.'

From What Kinds of Families Do Early Readers Come?

The families of the two groups of children were not nearly so similar. When the families were interviewed, differences that would be relevant to the research were identified. These differences were reported and discussed in Chapter VIII. Here, only a few will be mentioned again.

One very relevant difference was the attitude of the parents toward a matter like helping preschool children with reading. As might be expected, parents of the early readers showed greater willingness to give early help. They also showed less tendency to believe that reading should be taught only by a trained person. A most important factor here, however, was their additional belief that a child's own interest in becoming a reader lessens the need for special training on the part of a person who might help.

From family interview data it appeared that most of the parental help which led to a child's early reading ability was given in response to the child's questions and requests for assistance. On the other hand, it was surprising to hear that a third of the non-early-readers who showed preschool interest in reading received no help from their parents.

It must also be pointed out in this summary that when parents of the non-early-readers did help with reading, the help sometimes resulted from their own decision rather than from a child's curiosity and interest. The research seems to indicate, however, that young children are much more responsive to help with reading that is the consequence of their own questions rather than of their parents' ambition or insecurity—or whatever it is that prompts parents to make an arbitrary decision to teach preschoolers to read, without regard for the child's interest or for the possibility of strain developing in the parent–child relationship. The very special importance of the child's own interest needs to be high-lighted in the 1960's because, as previous chapters have pointed out, commercial pressure in this decade is pushing parents to invest in materials for teaching reading at home. If nothing else, findings from the two studies reported in this monograph clearly demonstrate that the everyday world of a preschool child is replete with opportunities to begin to learn to read, without the aid of teaching kits but with the help of parents who are more concerned about the children's interests than about their own ambitions.

Here, the influence of siblings in earlier reading must not be over-looked. The studies demonstrated that sibling help, especially in the form of "playing school," is very productive, but also that the probability of sibling help with reading depends upon the age difference between a preschooler and the next oldest child in his family. The smaller the age difference, the greater the likelihood of sibling help—particularly when the next older sibling is a girl.

One other factor should be mentioned in this very quick summary of findings about families of early readers and non-early-readers. It is the factor of socioeconomic class and its effect upon the likelihood of preschool reading.

In the first study, a preponderance of the early readers came from "blue collar" families. In that study, the few middle-class parents who were interviewed showed concern about problems that might ensue from the preschool achievement of their children. Thus, their views reflected beliefs widely held in 1958 about reading that begins "too soon."

By 1961, when the second study began, these beliefs had changed; so too had the views of some of the better-educated parents of the New York early readers. Whether this difference in parental attitude reflects the change in the locale of the research from the West Coast to the East, or indicates that better-educated parents are more aware and accepting of current beliefs about the growth and development of children, is not known. Perhaps the difference is rooted in both factors. But in either case, research findings show no simple connection between early reading and the socioeconomic status of a family. What is much more important, the research data indicated, is the presence of parents who spend time with their children; who read to them; who answer their questions and their requests for help; and who demonstrate in their own lives that reading is a rich source of relaxation, information, and contentment. Whether these same kinds of factors also helped to pro-mote the continued high achievement of the early readers in later grades was not studied. However, the possibility of their positive influence can-not be overlooked.

How Do Children Learn to Read at Home?

Implications of the research data for school programs will be made very explicit in what is to be the second phase of this research with pre-first-grade achievement in reading. The second phase will be a two-year language arts program for four- and five-year-old children. It will be an experimental attempt to incorporate into a school program certain characteristics and features suggested by data from this present research about the ways children learn to read at home. These data will be restated here as comprising six main findings:

1. The approach to reading of preschool children can be portrayed most accurately by what professional educators would call a language arts approach. ,Research findings indicated that for more than half of the early readers in California, and again in New York, interest in learning to print developed prior to, or simultaneously with, an interest in learning to read. In fact, for some early readers, ability to read seemed almost like a by-product of ability to print and to spell. For these "pencil and paper kids," the learning sequence moved from (a) scribbling and drawing, to (b) copying objects and letters of the alphabet, to (c) questions about spelling, to (d) ability to read.

2. One consequence of a child's ability to print was the asking of many questions about the spelling of particular words. Almost inevitably the initial request of the child was, "Show me my name." Generally, for their writing and drawing, children used paper and pencils—ordinary pencils, not the extra-thick ones still found in many primary grade classrooms. The early readers were also reported to have used small blackboards.

3. A child's persistent interest in writing and spelling sometimes encouraged a parent, or an older sibling, to talk about the sounds of letters. Sometimes this help was productive, sometimes not. However, when help with letter sounds was given, it was usually directed toward independence in spelling rather than reading.

4. Discussions with parents about the preschool scribbling and writing of their children disclosed what might be called "interest binges." Repeatedly the children were described as having had interests which were indulged in for long periods of time, then suddenly discarded. In one case, a mother said her daughter had gone through a stage in which she did nothing but copy people's names and addresses. In another home, an early reader had spent weeks making and remaking calendars. The sustained projects of these children were in striking contrast to the schedules of school programs which constantly interrupt young children because, it is said, the children have a short attention span.

5. A child's questions of "What does that word say?" seem to have been stimulated in a variety of ways. One frequent source of interest in whole words was the experience of being read to by a parent or an older sibling. Stories which were read and reread were generally the ones that led to such questions as "Where does it say that?" or "What's that word?" Other important sources of interest in whole words were television programs—especially commercials, quiz programs, and weather reports. Important, too, were the words found on such places as outdoor signs, food packages, menus, phonograph records, and cars and trucks.

6. A study of the way an early interest in reading develops also resulted in the identification of what might be called feminine *vs.* mascu-

line approaches to reading—at least in the matter of vocabulary. For instance, it was not uncommon to find that early entries in the boys' reading vocabularies included such words as *rocket, jet,* and *Chevrolet.* On the other hand, names of food products seemed to have special appeal for girls because of their importance when the girls played house or store.

Other Findings Related to
the Research

To end this chapter with a summary of research findings would be to bring down the curtain before the play has ended; for learnings accumulated in doing this research were hardly confined to formal, structured data. The "extra" learnings sometimes came from the planned procedures used to collect data for the two studies; this was especially true of the family interviews. Often, though, unanticipated learnings resulted from opportunities that were a by-product of the research. These included many invitations to speak at conferences throughout the country and to do consulting work in a wide variety of school systems. A quick summary of some learnings from these different sources follows.

First, in doing the research itself, it became clear that early readers are not a special brand of children who can be readily identified and sorted by tests. Rather, it would seem, it is their mothers who play the key role in effecting the early achievement. The homes they provide, the example they show, the time they give to the children, their concepts of their role as educator of the preschool child—all of these dimensions of home life and of parent–child relationships appeared to be of singular importance to the early reading achievement described in this report. Yet, apparent in many of the research interviews were much confusion and concern about what parents should and should not do regarding preschool help with "academic" learnings.

In a sense, such confusion and concern are to be expected in the 1960's. Over a very short period of time, popular beliefs about the potential of young children, and about the role of the parent in teaching the more academic skills, have changed radically. What is unfortunate is that professional educators now offer to parents only more confusion and, very often, much conflict.

If the kindergartens of today reflect professional opinion about education for young children, then the only possible conclusion is that wide diversity prevails among professional beliefs about the best way to educate the young. At one extreme are school systems in which kindergarten programs are duplicate copies of what they were as many as thirty years ago; in certain school systems this writer has even found that materials like pencils and paper are officially forbidden for the kindergartens because five-year-olds are not yet "ready" for them.

But other kinds of kindergartens, representing other extremes, have been visited too. Most often these extremes are to be found in areas in which earlier reading has taken on status value. In general, these areas are suburban communities in which the drive to achieve is so dominant as to be psychologically suffocating. The influence of overly ambitious parents, combined, perhaps, with insecure school administration, has resulted in kindergarten programs which look like a good imitation of a poor first-grade program. This writer has visited kindergartens which could be described quickly but completely by saying that they are cluttered with workbooks and noisy with phonics.

Fortunately—and these experiences insert hope into the somewhat dismal picture drawn thus far—this writer has also had the opportunity to consult with many kindergarten teachers and elementary school principals who clearly recognize the inadequacy of traditional programs but are also aware that the solution to the kindergarten problem is neither simple nor single. Hopefully, in the years to come, these educators will demonstrate that a middle-of-the-road position is not necessarily one that is dominated by compromise—that it may, rather, be characterized by a flexibility which takes its direction from the fact that five-year-olds show great variation in what they already know and in what they can and want to do.

Obviously, kindergartens that are to provide this flexibility will not develop automatically or with ease. And they can hardly even begin to emerge until certain basic questions have been given careful and informed thought. For example: What is the function of the total kindergarten program in the 1960's? It is both safe and sensible to assume that different communities will find different answers to this most fundamental of questions. It is probably safe to assume, too, that some of the answers will include help with reading for some five-year-olds. If this is the case, it is the sincere hope of this writer that findings from these two studies of early readers will provide at least a small amount of guidance in making decisions about what is appropriate help for five-year-old children who are ready to read.

References

References

1. Almy, Millie C. *Children's Experiences Prior to First Grade and Success in Beginning Reading.* New York: Bureau of Publications, Teachers College, Columbia University, 1949.

2. Anastasi, Anne. *Psychological Testing.* New York: The Macmillan Company, 1961.

3. Anonymous. "An Experiment in Infant Education," *Journal of Applied Psychology.* 2 (September, 1918), 219–228.

4. Appleton, Edith. "Kindergarteners Pace Themselves in Reading," *Elementary School Journal.* 64 (February, 1964), 248–252.

5. Ausubel, David P. "Viewpoints from Related Disciplines: Human Growth and Development," *Teachers College Record.* 60 (February, 1959), 245–254.

6. Ausubel, David P. "Learning by Discovery: Rationale and Mystique," *The Bulletin.* 45 (December, 1961), 18–58.

7. Benton, William. *This Is the Challenge.* New York: Associated College Presses, 1958.

8. Berry, Frances M. "The Baltimore Reading Readiness Test," *Childhood Education.* 3 (January, 1927), 222–223.

9. Bestor, Arthur E. *Educational Wastelands, the Retreat from Learning in Our Public Schools.* Urbana: University of Illinois Press, 1953.

10. Blake, P. "Long Research and the Happy Payoff," *Life.* 56 (April 3, 1964), 88–89.

11. Bloom, Benjamin S. *Stability and Change in Human Characteristics.* New York: John Wiley and Sons, 1964.

12. Brown, Muriel W. *A Study of Reading Ability in Preschool Children.* Unpublished master's thesis, Stanford University, 1924.

13. Bruner, Jerome. *The Process of Education.* Cambridge: Harvard University Press, 1960.

14. Brunsman, Howard S. *Census of Population: 1950.* Volume 2. Washington: United States Government Printing Office, 1952.

15. Buder, Leonard. "Schools Will End Group I.Q. Testing," *New York Times.* March 3, 1964, 36.

16. Burke, O. "Whitby School," *Jubilee.* 6 (February, 1959), 21–27.

17. Butler, A. L. "Hurry! Hurry! Hurry! Why?" *Childhood Education.* 39 (September, 1962), 10–13.

18. Coghill, G. E. *Anatomy and the Problem of Behavior.* Cambridge: Cambridge University Press, 1929.

19. Cole, Luella. *The Improvement of Reading.* New York: Farrar and Rinehart, 1938.

20. Cremin, Lawrence A. *The Transformation of the School.* New York: Alfred A. Knopf, 1961.

21. Davidson, Helen P. "An Experimental Study of Bright, Average, and Dull Children at the Four-Year Mental Level," *Genetic Psychology Monographs.* 9 (March, 1931), 119–287.

22. Deputy, E. C., *Predicting First-Grade Reading Achievement.* New York: Bureau of Publications, Teachers College, Columbia University, 1930.

23. Deutsch, Martin. "The Disadvantaged Child and the Learning Process." In A. H. Passow (Ed.), *Education in Depressed Areas.* New York: Teachers College Press, Teachers College, Columbia University, 1963.

24. Deutsch, Martin. "Papers from the Arden House Conference on Preschool Enrichment," *Merrill–Palmer Quarterly.* 10 (July, 1964), 207–208.

25. Dickson, Virgil E. *Mental Tests and the Classroom Teacher.* New York: World Book Company, 1923.

26. Doman, G., Stevens, G. L., and Orem, R. C. "You Can Teach Your Baby to Read," *Ladies Home Journal.* 80 (May, 1963), 62ff.

27. Editorial. "Crisis in Education," *Life.* 44 (March 24, 1958), 26–35.

28. Education Section. "O. K.'s Children," *Time.* 76 (November 7, 1960), 103.

29. Educational Policies Commission. *Contemporary Issues in Elementary Education.* Washington, D. C.: National Education Association, 1960.

30. Fouracre, M. H., Connor, F. P., and Goldberg, I. I. *The Effects of a Preschool Program upon Young Educable Mentally Retarded Children.* United States Office of Education Report, 1962. (The curriculum developed as part of this comprehensive study: Connor, F. P., and Talbot, M. E. *An Experimental Curriculum for Young Mentally Retarded Children.* New York: Teachers College Press, Teachers College, Columbia University, 1964.)

31. Gates, Arthur I. "The Necessary Mental Age for Beginning Reading," *Elementary School Journal.* 37 (March, 1937), 497–508.

32. Gates, Arthur I. Teacher's Manuals for the *Gates Reading Tests.* New York: Bureau of Publications, Teachers College, Columbia University, 1958.

33. Gates, A. I., and Bond, Guy. "Reading Readiness: A Study of Factors Determining Success and Failure in Beginning Reading," *Teachers College Record.* 37 (May, 1936), 679–685.

34. Gates, A. I., Bond, G. L., and Russell, D. H. *Methods of Determining Reading Readiness.* New York: Bureau of Publications, Teachers College, Columbia University, 1939.

35. Gesell, Arnold L. *The Mental Growth of the Preschool Child.* New York: The Macmillan Company, 1925.

36. Gesell, Arnold L. *Infancy and Human Growth.* New York: The Macmillan Company, 1928.

37. Gesell, Arnold L. "The Ontogenesis of Infant Behavior." In L. Carmichael (Ed.), *Manual of Child Psychology.* New York: John Wiley and Sons, 1954.

38. Gesell, A., and Ilg, F. *The Child from Five to Ten.* New York: Harper and Brothers, 1946.

39. Getsels, J. W., and Jackson, P. W. "The Meaning of 'Giftedness'—An Examination of an Expanding Concept," *Phi Delta Kappan.* 40 (November, 1958), 75–77.

40. Golann, S. E. "Psychological Study of Creativity," *Psychological Bulletin.* 60 (November, 1963), 548–565.

41. Hall, G. Stanley. *The Psychology of Adolescence.* New York: D. Appleton and Company, 1904.

42. Harrison, M. Lucille. *Reading Readiness.* Boston: Houghton Mifflin Company, 1936.

43. Havighurst, Robert. *Human Development and Education.* New York: Longmans, Green, and Company, 1953.

44. Heffernan, Helen. "Significance of Kindergarten Education," *Childhood Education.* 36 (March, 1960), 313–319.

45. Hillman, Rosemary. "In Defense of the Five-Year-Old," *Saturday Review.* 46 (November 16, 1963), 77ff.

46. Holmes, Margaret C. "Investigation of Reading Readiness of First Grade Entrants," *Childhood Education.* 3 (January, 1927), 215–221.

47. Huey, Edmund B. *The Psychology and Pedagogy of Reading.* New York: The Macmillan Company, 1908.

48. Hunt, J. McVicker. *Intelligence and Experience.* New York: The Ronald Press Company, 1961.

49. Hunt, J. McVicker. "The Psychological Basis for Using Preschool Enrichment As an Antidote for Cultural Deprivation," *Merrill–Palmer Quarterly.* 10 (July, 1964), 209–248.

50. Hutt, M. L., and Briskin, G. J. *The Clinical Use of the Revised Bender Gestalt Test.* New York: Grune and Stratton, 1960.

51. Hymes, J. L. "The Importance of Pre-primary Education," *Childhood Education.* 39 (September, 1962), 5–9.

52. Hymes, J. L. "More Pressure for Early Reading," *Childhood Education.* 40 (September, 1963), 34–35.

53. Ilg, F., and Bates, L. "Developmental Trends in Reading Behavior," *Journal of Genetic Psychology.* 76 (June, 1950), 291–312.

54. Jenkins, Frances. "Editorial," *Childhood Education.* 3 (January, 1927), 209.

55. Kasdon, Lawrence M. "Early Reading Background of Some Superior Readers among College Freshmen," *Journal of Educational Research.* 52 (December, 1958), 151–153.

56. Keister, B. V. "Reading Skills Acquired by Five-Year-Old Children," *Elementary School Journal.* 41 (April, 1941), 587–596.

57. Kelley, M. L. "When Are Children 'Ready' to Read?" *Saturday Review.* 46 (July 20, 1963), 58ff.

58. Kelly, T. L., *et al. Stanford Achievement Test.* New York: World Book Company, 1953.

59. Kirk, Samuel A. *Early Education of the Mentally Retarded: An Experimental Study.* Urbana, Illinois: University of Illinois Press, 1958.

60. Kuhlmann, F., and Anderson, Rose G. *Kuhlmann–Anderson Mental Test* (Seventh Edition). Princeton, New Jersey: Personnel Press, 1952.

61. Lamoreaux, L. A., and Lee, D. M. *Learning to Read through Experience.* New York: Appleton–Century–Crofts, 1943.

62. Lindberg, L., and Moffitt, M. W. "The Program and the Child," *National Elementary Principal.* 40 (September, 1960), 50–125.

63. McCarthy, Dorothea. "Language Development in Children." In L. Carmichael (Ed.), *Manual of Child Psychology.* New York: John Wiley and Sons, 1954.

64. McCracken, Glenn. "Have We Overemphasized Readiness?" *Elementary English.* 29 (May, 1952), 271–276.

65. McCracken, Glenn. "The Newcastle Reading Experiment," *"Elementary English.* 30 (January, 1953), 13–21.

66. McCracken, Glenn. "The Newcastle Reading Experiment," *Elementary School Journal.* 54 (March, 1954), 385–390.

67. McCracken, Glenn. *The Right to Learn.* Chicago: Henry Regnery Company, 1959.

68. McGraw, Myrtle B. *Growth: A Study of Johnny and Jimmy.* New York: D. Appleton–Century Company, 1935.

69. Mayne, Lucille. "An Individual Study of the Reading Acceleration of Two Kindergarten Children," *Elementary English.* 40 (April, 1963), 406–408.

70. Mead, Margaret. "Questions That Need Asking," *Teachers College Record.* 63 (November, 1961), 89–93.

71. Milner, Esther. "A Study of the Relationship between Reading Readiness in Grade One School Children and Patterns of Parent–Child Interaction," *Child Development.* 22 (June, 1951), 95–112.

72. Montessori, Maria. *The Montessori Method.* Cambridge, Massachusetts: Robert Bentley, Inc., 1964.

73. Morphett, M. V., and Washburne, C. "When Should Children Begin to Read?" *Elementary School Journal.* 31 (March, 1931), 496–503.

74. Morris, J. A. "Can Our Children Learn Faster?" *The Saturday Evening Post.* 234 (September 23, 1961), 17–25.

75. National Society for the Study of Education. *The Twenty-fourth Yearbook of the NSSE,* Part I. Bloomington, Illinois: Public School Publishing Co., 1925.

76. Olson, Willard. *Child Development.* Boston: D. C. Heath and Company, 1949.

77. Olson, W., and Hughes, B. "Concepts of Growth," *Childhood Education,* 21 (October, 1944), 53–63.

78. Partridge, G. E. *Genetic Philosophy of Education.* New York: Sturgis and Walton Company, 1912.

79. Pines, Maya. "How Three-Year-Olds Teach Themselves to Read—and Love It," *Harper's Magazine.* 226 (May, 1963), 58–64.

80. Pintner, R., Cunningham, B., and Durost, W. *Pintner-Cunningham Primary Test.* Yonkers, New York: World Book Company, 1938.

81. Polhemus, Mary E. "Home–School Cooperation for Better Readers," *Elementary English*. 32 (November, 1955), 461–465.

82. Pruette, Lorine. *G. Stanley Hall: A Biography of a Mind*. New York: Appleton, 1926.

83. Rambusch, Nancy McC. *Learning How to Learn*. Baltimore: Helicon Press, 1962.

84. Rasmussen, Margaret (Editor). *Reading in the Kindergarten?* Washington, D. C.: Association for Childhood Education International, 1962.

85. Reed, Mary M. *An Investigation of Practices in First Grade Admission and Promotion*. New York: Bureau of Publications, Teachers College, Columbia University, 1927.

86. Sheldon, William D. "Should the Very Young Be Taught to Read?" *NEA Journal*. 52 (November, 1963), 20–22.

87. Sheldon, W. D., and Carrillo, L. "Relation of Parents, Home, and Certain Developmental Characteristics to Children's Reading Ability," *Elementary School Journal*. 52 (January, 1952), 262–270.

88. Simmons, Virginia C. "Why Waste Our Five-Year-Olds?" *Harper's Magazine*. 220 (April, 1960), 71–73.

89. Smith, Nila B. "Matching Ability As a Factor in First Grade Reading," *Journal of Educational Psychology*. 19 (November, 1928), 560–571.

90. Strang, Ruth. "Reading Development of Gifted Children," *Elementary English*. 31 (January, 1954), 35–40.

91. Sutton, M. H. "Readiness for Reading at the Kindergarten Level," *Reading Teacher*. 17 (January, 1964), 234–240.

92. Terman, Lewis M. *Genetic Studies of Genius*. Vol. 1. Stanford, Cal.: Stanford University Press, 1925.

93. Thorndike, E. L. *The Psychology of Learning*. New York: Bureau of Publications, Teachers College, Columbia University, 1923.

94. Thorndike, R. L., and Hagen, E. *Measurement and Evaluation in Psychology and Education*. New York: John Wiley and Sons, 1961.

95. Tomlinson, Ethel. "Language Arts Skills Needed by Lower Class Children," *Elementary English*. 33 (May, 1956), 279–283.

96. Torrance, E. Paul. *Minnesota Tests of Creative Thinking*, Abbreviated Form VII. University of Minnesota, Bureau of Educational Research, 1962.

97. Van Wie, E. K., and Lammers, D. M. "Are We Being Fair to Our Kindergartners?" *Elementary School Journal*. 52 (April, 1962), 348–351.

98. Warner, W. L., Meeker, M., and Eels, K. *Social Class in America*. Chicago: Science Research Associates, 1949.

99. Watson, John B. *Behaviorism*. New York: W. W. Norton and Company, 1924.

100. Watson, John. *Psychological Care of Infant and Child*. New York: W. W. Norton Company, 1928.

101. Weisman, Dorothy. "Is Play Obsolete?" *Saturday Review*. 46 (November 16, 1963), 77ff.

102. Wilson, Frank T. "Reading Progress in Kindergarten and Primary Grades," *Elementary School Journal*. 38 (February, 1938), 442–449.

Appendices

Appendix A. The Test Used to Identify Early Readers

NAME _____ SCHOOL _____

said	to	down	jump
mother	for	big	house
red	it	in	blue
want	father	here	we
can	is	work	away
help	stop	little	ball
get	and	funny	you
the	come	play	see
look	make	me	go
			not

The ball is red.

Come and look.

Come and see the ball.

It is not big.

It is little and red.

Mother said it is for me.

In the test form used by the children, the lettering was similar to the type used here, but larger (about 18-point).

Appendix B. California Family Questionnaire

Name: Date of Interview:

FAMILY BACKGROUND

Father

Birthplace:
High school graduate?
College graduate?   Graduate work?
Occupation:
  Father's occupation:
Did your husband ever want to be a teacher?
  (If so) Explain:
Does your husband belong to any school organizations?
  (If so) Explain:
How often does he get to school?

Mother

Birthplace:
High school graduate?
College graduate?   Graduate work?
Occupation:
  (If housewife) before marriage:
  Father's occupation:
Did you ever want to be a teacher?
  (If so) Explain:
Do you belong to any school organizations?
  (If so) Explain:
How often do you go to school?

Siblings

  Brother(s):   Sister(s):
  Ages: Ages:

Home

Do any adults live here, other than you and your husband?
  (If so) Who?
Languages spoken in home:
By whom?
Physical description of home and neighborhood:

153

SUBJECT

Birthplace: Date:

What illnesses has your son (daughter) had?
  [Illnesses listed, with ages and durations]
Has your son (daughter) ever had any problems with his (her) eyes?
  (If so) Explain:
Does he (she) ever complain about his (her) eyes now?
  (If so) Explain:
Have you ever had to take him (her) to an eye doctor?
  (If so) Explain:
At what age did your son (daughter) begin to walk?
At what age did he (she) begin to talk?
Did your son (daughter) go to nursery school?
  (If so) Kind:
      Duration:
Why did you send him (her) to nursery school?
Did you son (daughter) attend kindergarten?
  (If so) Kind:
      Duration:
Why did you send him (her) to kindergarten?
Did your son (daughter) like kindergarten?
  Why? (Why not?)
What did your son (daughter) learn in kindergarten?
Were you satisfied with what your son (daughter) got out of kindergarten?
  Why? (Why not?)
What does the kindergarten at your school try to accomplish with the children?
Did it accomplish this for your son (daughter)?
  Explain:
How did he (she) feel about starting first grade?
How has he (she) felt about his (her) teachers? What about his (her) kindergarten
  teacher?
How does he (she) feel now about his (her) first grade teacher?
Has your child ever said he (she) didn't want to go to school? To kindergarten, for
  instance?
  Explain:
Thus far, has there been a day when he (she) didn't want to go to first grade?
  Explain:
Is he (she) the kind of child who would worry about his (her) progress in school?
  Explain:

OTHER INFORMATION

How does he (she) compare with his (her) older sister(s) and brother(s) . . .
  In academic ability?
  In motor skills?
Did any of your other children learn to read before they started first grade?
  (If so) Which one(s)?
Have any of your children had problems learning to read?
  (If so) Explain:
Do you help the older children with their homework?
  (If so) Which one(s)?
      When?
      Where?
      With what in particular?

Does your husband help the older children with their homework?
(If so) Which one(s)?
      When?
      Where?
      With what in particular?
Was (name subject) ever around when this help with homework was being given?
(If so) Describe:
Did any of the older children read to (name subject) before he (she) started kindergarten?
(If so) Which one(s)?
      How often?
      Materials?
      Procedure:
Did your husband read to him (her) before he (she) started kindergarten?
(If so) How often?
      Materials?
      Procedure:
What about the reading your husband does himself? Would you say he reads more than the average adult?
      [Reading materials and frequencies listed]
Did you read to (name subject) before he (she) started kindergarten?
(If so) How often?
      Materials?
      Procedure:
Did anybody else read to him (her)?
(If so) Who?
      How often?
      Materials?
      Procedure:
When was your child first read to at home?
What about your own reading? Would you say you read more than the average adult?
      [Reading materials and frequencies listed]
When you go out with your children, where do you generally take them?
Does (name subject) like to play?   With whom?
What do they especially like to do?
What kind of play was of special interest to your child before he (she) started kindergarten?
Does (name subject) watch television?
      Frequency: Kinds of programs:
Did he (she) watch more often, or less often, before starting first grade?
      Frequency then:

EARLY READING AND WRITING

Reading
    At what age did your son (daughter) first show an interest in written words or numbers?
    How did he (she) show the interest?
    Can you remember what might have encouraged the interest?
    Explain:
    What do you have around the house that might encourage a young child's interest in reading?
    As you look back to the earlier years of your son (daughter), what would you say was especially important in stimulating his (her) early interest in reading?
    In your family, or even outside the family, what did people do to help your child learn to read early? What kinds of help did they give him (her)?

Can you think of anything else?

Just to be sure nothing has been omitted, I wonder whether you could tell me again who it was who helped your child, and the kinds of help he gave.

[Persons and kinds of help listed]

What materials were used by each of these people?

[Persons listed, with materials used]

Why did each of these people give the help?

[Persons and reasons listed]

Of these people, who was the one who seemed to teach your child the most about reading?

As you look back to all of the various kinds of help given to your son (daughter), could you tell me with what frequency it was given? For example, would you say that once (name subject) showed an interest in learning to read, he (she) then got help everyday? In your own words, how would you describe the frequency of this preschool help?

Does your son (daughter) go to the library now?

(If "Yes") When did he (she) begin going to the library?

(If "No") Did you ever take him (her) to the library when he (she) was younger?

Explain:

Printing

Is your son (daughter) right-handed or left-handed?

Does he (she) do different things with different hands?

(If so) Explain:

Could your child print when he (she) sharted first grade?

(If so) Could you give me some idea of how well he (she) could print then?

(If not) Did he (she) ever show any interest in trying to print?

Explain:

(If so) At what age did he (she) first show an interest in learning to print?

At what age did he (she) actually do some printing?

What got this interest started?

Who actually helped him (her) learn to print?

[Persons and procedures listed]

SUMMARY INFORMATON

Do you think parents should give help, with things like reading, to preschool children?

Why? (Why not?)

Let's take reading in particular. Do you think reading ought to be taught only by a trained person?

Why? (Why not?)

Do you think the schools are doing a good job teaching children to read?

Explain:

As you know, I don't know (name subject). How would you describe your son (daughter) in terms of his (her) temperament and attitudes? For example, in what ways is he (she) either like other children, or different from them? What words would best describe him (her)?

I don't know your child. Are there any other words that would help me to know the kind of child he (she) is?

Appendix C. New York Family Questionnaire and Response Frequencies

Name: Date:

I. FAMILY BACKGROUND

Father

Birthplace: U. S. (77—90)[1]
                Foreign born (23—10)

Elementary school graduate?	Yes (100—100)	No (0—0)
High school?	Yes (97—90)	No (3—10)
College?	Yes (37—50)	No (63—50)
Graduate work?	Yes (17—7)	No (83—93)

Occupation:
Grandfather's occupation:
Foreign born? Yes (70—83)   No (30—17)

Mother

Birthplace: U. S. (83—93)
                Foreign born (17—7)

Elementary school graduate?	Yes (100—100)	No (0—0)
High school?	Yes (90—80)	No (10—20)
College?	Yes (33—10)	No (67—90)
Graduate work?	Yes (7—7)	No (93—93)

Occupation:
    (If housewife) Before marriage:
Did you ever want to become a teacher? Yes (17—13)   No (83—87)
Grandfather's occupation:
Foreign born? Yes (63—72)   No (37—28)

II. HOME

Membership

Any adults other than parents? Yes (3—0)   No (97—100)
    Who?

[1] The numbers shown for response categories are percentages. The first describes the frequency of a response in the interviews with parents of the early readers; the second, the frequency for the non-early-readers. For example, 77 per cent of the fathers of early readers, and 90 per cent of the fathers of non-early-readers, were born in the United States.

157

Siblings: [Number]   [Age]
  Older brother(s):
  Younger brother(s):
  Older sister(s):
  Younger sister(s):
      (Total):

Language   Second language (if any):
  Monolingual (100—87)   Spoken by:
  Bilingual (0—13)   When:
Physical Description:

III. SUBJECT

Birthplace
Date
At what age did child begin to walk? [2]   Talk?
  (27—40) before   one year   (13—20 before one year
  (70—40) about one year   (40—23) about one year
  (3—17) about 18 mos.   (33—20) about 18 mos.
  (0—3) about 2 years   (10—23) about 2 years
  (0—0) later (   )   (3—13) later (   )
Is child left-handed or right-handed? L. (27—27) R. (73—73)
Does he do different things with different hands? Yes (0—0) No (100—100)
  (If so) Explain:
What illnesses has child had?
  [Illnesses listed, with ages and durations]
Has child ever had problems with his eyes? Yes (0—0) No (100—100)
  (If so) Explain:
Have you ever had to take him to an eye doctor? Yes (0—0) No (100—100)
  (If so) Explain:
Does he ever complain about his eyes now? Yes (0—0) No (100—100)
  (If so) Explain:

Preschool Play

When playing, how much energy did child have compared to children his age?
  (60—60) more than average
  (40—37) average
  (0—3) less than average
In what types of activities did child do especially well?
  (27—43) outdoor, active games
  (10—13) work with tools; building
  (40—30) fine handwork; art
  (63—37) quiet games; checkers, cards, etc.
  (27—13) other (specify)
When no other children were available, what did child usually do to occupy his time?
  (97—83) looked at books, magazines, etc.
  (23—27) made things with hands
  (7—40) played with toys, balls, etc.
  (23—27) watched television
  (3—0) tried to get an adult's attention
  (0—0) loafed around, wondering what to do
  (23—17) other (specify)

[2] In an interview, the subject's name was used in place of "child."

With whom did child usually play?
    (83—73) children his own age
    (7—13) younger children
    (23—30) older children
    (20—13) siblings
When child played with other children, what did they usually do?
    (67—77) played active games
    (70—43) played quiet games
    (13—17) made things
    (23—20) played school
    (13—13) played with books; scissors; crayons; paper and pencil, etc.
    (0—0) other (specify)
Did child prefer to spend time with adults or with children?
    (7—0) adults
    (67—73) children
    (23—27) both
    (3—0) liked to spend time alone
Did child like to play alone? Yes (80—37)   No (20—63)
    (If so) What did he do?

IV. SIBLING RELATIONSHIPS

How does child compare with (brother) and/or (sister) in academic or intellectual ability? [3]
    (55—43) better
    (36—46) same
    (9—11) less able
Do the children compete with each other? Yes (68—57)   No (32—43)
    Describe:

V. SCHOOL

Nursery School
Did child attend nursery school? Yes (43—30)   No (57—70)
    (If so) Which one?
        For how long?
          (0—0) 3 years
          (15—44) 2 years
          (62—56) 1 year
          (23—0) less
Why did you send child to nursery school?
    (62—67) He needed to be with other children.
    (15—11) I worked.
    (16—22) Other children were going.
    (23—22) It is a good preparation for school.
    (0—0) Other (specify)
How did he benefit from nursery school?
    (62—60) learned to play with other children
    (39—60) learned songs; rhymes; games; etc.
    (8—0) developed interest in reading; printing
    (23—44) learned to relate to other adult
    (39—33) learned how to behave in school setting
    (0—0) Other (specify)

[3] Because of one-child families in the research, this and the following question were asked in 22 early reader interviews and in 28 non-early-reader interviews.

Did child ever say he wanted to stay home? Yes (100—100) No (0—0)
  (If so) How often?
                    (39—78) only in the beginning
                    (62—22) intermittently
                    (0—0) most of the time
Did child watch any nursery-school–kindergarten-type programs on television?
  Yes (60—80) No (40—20)
  (If so) What did he learn from them?

Kindergarten

Did child go to kindergarten? Yes (97—100) No (3—0)
  (If so) Which one?
              For how long?
                    (100—100) 1 year
                    (0—0) 1 semester
                    (0—0) less
              Why did you send him?
                    (0—0) He needed to be with other children.
                    (7—3) I worked.
                    (100—100) It's the usual thing to do.
                    (0—0) It's a good preparation for first grade.
                    (0—0) other (specify)
What did child learn in kindergarten?
  (79—83) learned to play with other children
  (45—53) learned songs; rhymes; games; etc.
  (0—0) developed an interest in reading; printing; etc.
  (0—0) learned to read; print; etc.
  (55—53) learned how to behave in school setting
  (0—0) other (specify)
Did child ever say he wanted to stay home? Yes (100—100) No (0—0)
  (If so) How often?
                    (55—70) only in the beginning
                    (45—30) intermittently
                    (0—0) most of the time

First Grade

Is child interested in first grade? Yes (60—87) No (40—13)
Let me be more specific. Which of the following describe child's interest in first
  grade?
  (20—73) extremely interested
  (40—13) adequately interested
  (40—13) sometimes he likes it; sometimes he doesn't
  (0—0) not at all interested
When child does show interest in first grade, what seems to be of special interest to
  him?
  (10—10) play periods
  (63—67) reading (or related areas)
  (27—33) arithmetic
  (33—30) art; music
  (10—3) other (specify)
Is child having any particular problems in first grade? Yes (0—0)
  (If so) Describe: No (100—100)
What do you feel is the most important thing to be learned in the first grade?
  (100—100) ability to read
  (47—40) skill in arithmetic
  (30—27) successful relationships with other children
  (3—0) other (specify)

Are you satisfied with what child is learning in first grade?
    (53—67) yes
    (23—27) no
    (23—7) uncertain

VI. OTHER ACTIVITIES

Does child attend any school other than the public school? Yes (50—57)
                                                 No (50—43)
  (If so) Describe:
Did child watch television before starting kindergarten? Yes (97—100)
                                               No (3—0)
  (If so) How often? [4]
                (28—7) 5 or fewer hours per week
                (31—37) 6—10 hours per week
                (24—23) 11—15 hours per week
                (14—13) 16—20 hours per week
                (3—10) 21—25 hours per week
                (0—10) 25 or more hours per week
Are you aware of any valuable learnings child acquired from watching television?
  (79—57) yes
  (21—33) no
  (3—10) uncertain
What were these learnings?
  (70—18) curiosity about written word
  (13—0) interest in learning to print
  (39—53) knowledge about history; science; etc.
  (9—29) other (specify)
Does your child go to the library? Yes (67—80)   No (33—20)
  (If so) How often?
                (40—25) once a week
                (30—29) once every two weeks
                (30—46) less often
Do you take out books from the library? Yes (83—33) No (17—67)
Does your husband? Yes (20—47)   No (80—53)
Do you read more than the average adult? Yes (83—33)   No (17—67)
Does your husband? Yes (17—33)   No (83—67)
Did you or anybody else read to child before he started school? Yes (100—73)
                                             No (0—27)
  (If so) Could you tell me how this reading was done?
                (80—41) told him words he asked about
                (17—36) checked his comprehension of the story
                (40—32) pointed out words while reading
                (73—68) discussed pictures
                (0—0) other
Now that he can read himself, do you still read to him? Yes (80—70)
                                          No (20—30)
  (If so) How often?
                (58—43) every day
                (21—43) couple times a week
                (17—10) less often
                (4—5) when he asks for it
Does he himself read at home? Yes (100—97) No (0—3)

---

[4] One family of an early reader did not own a television set. Consequently, this and the next two questions were not asked in that interview.

(If so) How often?
　　　　(93—80) every day
　　　　(7—10) couple times a week
　　　　(0—10) less often
Before child ever learned to read, what kinds of reading materials were available to
　　him?
　(23—30) basal readers
　(33—27) workbooks
　(70—53) library books
　(87—77) Golden books
　(70—63) coloring books
　(87—77) alphabet books

VII. PARENTAL ATTITUDES

Are you satisfied with the job the schools are doing in teaching reading?
　Yes (53—73)   No (47—27)
　Why (not)?
Do you think parents should give help with things like reading to a preschool
　child?   Yes (100—50)   No (0—50)
　(Yes)
　(83—87) if he is interested
　(10—0) gives him a good start in school
　(7—13) other (specify)
　(No)
　(0—20) He'll be in school long enough.
　(0—87) It might mix him up when he gets to school.
　(0—20) It might lessen his interest in school.
　(0—27) Teaching requires special training.

VIII. PRESCHOOL TEACHING AND LEARNING

Did your child show any preschool interest in learning to read?   Yes (100—73)
　　　　　　　　　　　　　　　　　　　　　　　　　　　　　　　　　　No (0—27)
What do you think are some of the things that interested your child in learning to
　read? [5]
　(87—68) being read to at home
　(73—59) interest in printing
　(57—41) interest in spelling
　(47—46) television commercials
　(73—82) curiosity about written words
　(47—9) interest in word meanings
　(73—14) availability of reading materials
　(83—18) availability of paper and pencils
　(57—23) availability of blackboard
　(23—23) wanting to keep up with older siblings
　(23—9) wanting to do homework with siblings
　(20—14) school work brought home by siblings
　(3—0) other (specify)
At what age did child first show this preschool interest in learning to read?
　(17—9) before 3 years
　(33—32) about 3 years
　(50—41) about 4 years
　(0—18) about 5 years
　(0—0) during kindergarten
　(0—0) during the summer prior to first grade

[5] This and the next two questions were asked only of the 52 parents who said
their children showed preschool interest in reading.

Did you or anybody else give child preschool help with reading? Yes (100—68)

No (0—32)

(If so) At which age:

        (17—9) before 3 years

        (33—32) about 3 years

        (50—41) about 4 years

        (0—18) about 5 years

        (0—0) during kindergarten

        (0—0) during the summer prior to first grade

(If not) Why not?

Would you tell me whether you or anybody else gave child the following kinds of help? [6]

Identified words?	Yes (91—27)	No (9—73)
Helped with printing?	Yes (93—73)	No (7—27)
Discussed sounds of letters?	Yes (67—27)	No (33—73)
Discussed meanings of words?	Yes (77—27)	No (23—73)
Identified numbers?	Yes (93—87)	No (7—13)
Identified letter names?	Yes (100—100)	No (0—0)
Helped with spelling?	Yes (73—27)	No (27—73)

Could you tell me why these various kinds of help were given?

(13—7) to teach him to read

(47—33) to keep him occupied

(83—67) to answer his questions

(0—0) other (specify)

Who were the people who gave child most of the preschool help with things like the identification of numbers and letters and words, or with printing and spelling, and so on?

(93—87) mother

(3—13) father

(7—0) brother

(13—27) sister

(10—7) other relatives (specify)

(0—0) friend (specify)

Do you think reading ought to be taught only by a trained person? Yes (30—70)

No (70—30)

Why (not)?

Did you have any special concerns about your child's early ability in reading? [7] Yes (17) No (83)

(If so) What were they?

        (100) thought it would lessen his interest in school

        (0) thought it would make him overly confident

        (0) thought the way he learned might be different from how he would be taught in school

        (0) other (specify)

IX. SIBLINGS AND READING

Did any of the older children in your family learn to read before they started school? [8] Yes (43—31) No (57—69)

(If so) Specify:

---

[6] This and the next two questions were asked only of the 45 parents who said preschool help with reading and related skills was given to their children.

[7] This question was asked only in interviews with the parents of early readers.

[8] This and the next two questions were asked only of the 33 families in which there was a child who was older than the research subject.

Did you give any of the older children in the family help at home with their school work?   Yes (79—74)   No (21—26)

Did child listen and watch while you gave the help?   Yes (54—71)   No (46—29)
(If so) How often?
- (67—40) all of the time
- (33—40) some of the time
- (0—20) very infrequently

X. PERSONALITY CHARACTERISTICS

During this interview you have used many different words to describe your child. Now I'd like to try to get a total picture of him. Could you tell me again the words that best describe your child?

If somebody else were to take care of your child, what would you feel was especially important for her to know about him?

Does your child have any characteristics which he showed as an infant, and which he still shows?

I have a list of words which might or might not describe your child. If a word does describe him accurately, would you put a check in front of it? If a word does not describe your child, leave the space blank. [On a separate sheet of paper, the following list was given to parents.]

- _____ good memory
- _____ persistent
- _____ curious
- _____ competitive
- _____ perfectionistic

[Next, the following request was made.]

Would you look over the list again? If there is any word in the list which is an absolutely perfect description of your child, would you put a double check in front of that word?

Appendix D. Teacher Rating Scale and Response Frequencies

Date

Please evaluate _____ _____ on the following abilities, traits, and attitudes as you have seen them displayed both in and out of the classroom. After examining all of the possible ratings for each question, please check the most appropriate one.

A. How intelligent is he? [1]

    1. (0—0) Extremely dull
    2. (0—1) Dull
    3. (3—15) Equal of average child
    4. (23—13) Very bright
    5. (4—1) Brilliant

B. How would you describe his memory?

    1. (0—0) Unusually poor
    2. (0—0) Below average
    3. (2—12) Average for child his age
    4. (15—14) Above average
    5. (13—4) Amazingly good

C. Is he easily discouraged, or is he persistent?

    1. (0—0) Quits immediately before slight obstacles
    2. (2—1) Quits before adequate trial
    3. (11—20) Gives everything a fair trial
    4. (17—9) Is more persistent than most children
    5. (0—0) Never gives up; extremely persistent

D. Is he competitive?

    1. (1—0) Shows absolutely no interest in doing better than other children
    2. (4—7) Seldom strives; does the minimum
    3. (17—22) Attempts to do his best
    4. (7—1) Strives to do better than others
    5. (1—0) Feels he must always outdo and excel others

E. How are his work habits?

    1. (2—0) Extremely careless
    2. (1—1) Indifferent
    3. (7—13) Shows average care for child his age
    4. (14—15) Very careful
    5. (6—1) Inclined to be a perfectionist

[1] The first of the two numbers shown for each response category indicates the frequency with which that category was used to describe the early readers; the second is the frequency for the non-early-readers.

F. Is he self-reliant?

    1. (0—1) Depends completely on others
    2. (1—1) Most often dependent upon others
    3. (11—20) Shows average amount of independence and dependence for child his age
    4. (14—6) Most often independent of others
    5. (4—2) Extremely independent

G. In general, is his attention sustained as he works?

    1. (1—0) Very easily distracted
    2. (3—3) Difficult to keep at task until finished
    3. (4—10) Attends adequately for child his age
    4. (8—12) Becomes very absorbed in task
    5. (14—5) Able to concentrate for unusually long periods of time

H. Does he worry, or is he happy-go-lucky?

    1. (0—1) Entirely carefree; never worries about anything
    2. (5—4) Easy going
    3. (21—15) Does not worry without due cause
    4. (4—8) Often worries unduly
    5. (0—2) Constantly worrying; shows anxiety

I. Does he give in to other children, or does he assert himself?

    1. (1—0) Never asserts self; submissive
    2. (3—4) Generally gives in
    3. (22—23) Holds his own
    4. (5—2) Tends more to dominate than to give in
    5. (0—0) Always wants to dominate others

J. How would you describe his attitude toward adults?

    1. (0—0) Indifferent to adults
    2. (1—2) Shows minimum interest in pleasing adults
    3. (16—25) Shows average interest in pleasing adults
    4. (13—3) Displays more than average interest in pleasing adults
    5. (0—0) Overly eager to please adults

K. Is he a curious child?

    1. (0—0) Shows no curiosity about anything; is very indifferent
    2. (2—2) Occasionally displays some curiosity and interest
    3. (14—17) Displays usual curiosity and interest of child his age
    4. (12—11) Interests are easily aroused; asks more questions than other children
    5. (2—0) Is constantly asking questions about everything; extremely curious

L. How would you describe his speaking vocabulary?

    1. (1—0) Unusually limited for child his age
    2. (0—0) Below average
    3. (5—20) Average
    4. (15—7) Above average
    5. (9—3) Unusually extensive for child his age

M. How would you describe his ability to express ideas?

    1. (0—0) Unusually poor for child his age
    2. (1—1) Below average
    3. (6—15) Average
    4. (14—9) Above average
    5. (9—5) Remarkably good for child his age

Appendix E. Ratings Based on Bender Gestalt Test Data

Name _____ **Date** _____

Intelligence:	Very Slow			Very Bright
	(1)	(2)	(9)	(18)
	(1)	(2)	(9)	(18)

Memory:	Very Poor			Unusually Good
	(2)	(1)	(10)	(16)
	(3)	(5)	(9)	(14)

Persistence:	Gives Up Quickly			Never Gives Up
	(2)	(4)	(8)	(16)
	(4)	(4)	(8)	(14)

Work Habits:	Extremely Careless			Perfectionistic
	(4)	(3)	(12)	(11)
	(3)	(6)	(7)	(14)

Self-Reliance:	Completely Dependent			Completely Independent
	(1)	(15)	(11)	(3)
	(2)	(14)	(9)	(5)

Attention to Job:	Easily Distracted			Unusual Concentration
	(2)	(4)	(11)	(13)
	(3)	(6)	(7)	(14)

Tendency to Worry:	Extremely Easy-going			Constantly Worrying
	(1)	(13)	(14)	(2)
	(3)	(16)	(9)	(2)

Attitude toward Adults:	Very Indifferent			Very Eager to Please
	(1)	(13)	(16)	(0)
	(2)	(14)	(14)	(0)

Note: For each item, the numbers above the line indicate the distribution of ratings given the 30 early readers; the numbers below the line show the distribution for the 30 non-early-readers.

Index

Index